MW00817647

PRAISE FOR *KEEPING THE FAITH*

The letter written by Jude is often ignored today, and so I was delighted to see such a helpful and practical explanation of Jude's message. Davis shows that individuals, churches, and our culture can't afford to ignore the message of Jude, for we must pay attention to Jude's message to keep ourselves in God's love.

THOMAS R. SCHREINER
Professor and Associate Dean, The Southern Baptist Theological Seminary

Lianna has written a remarkable Bible study that is both deep and rich. It is a solid guide to help enlarge one's understanding of the call of God to fidelity to the truth of the gospel. It is beautifully written, with helpful commentary along with a thought-provoking study guide. Helpful quotes are included from theologians that enlarge the understanding of Jude's message. Mercy, peace, and love are core themes, but Lianna also hits the head on Jude's confrontational and convictional content that encourages believers, by God's grace, to contend for the faith. I loved this Bible study. I am deeply thankful for how it led me to worship and delight in the truth of the gospel of the Lord Jesus Christ. I highly commend it to you! This message is sorely needed for all believers.

PAMELA MACRAE
Professor and Program Chair for Ministry to Women, Moody Bible Institute

Jude is a short book, but Davis directs our eyes to gems we might have missed and peels back layers we might have ignored. Her careful attention to each phrase invites us to treasure God's Word, her lyrical writing guides us to savor each truth, and her theological insight leads us to marvel at the depth of this book. It is a journey not to be missed.

ARTHUR KOK
Equipping Ministry, Unlocking the Bible, and coauthor, *The New Elder's Handbook*

A necessary and crucial study for all believers. Lianna guides you through the words of Jude in a way that leads you to a greater depth of knowing the great richness of Christ as she teaches you why and how we must protect and defend our faith, holding fast to truth at all costs. A study I will no doubt go back to and encourage each of my disciples to go through.

LINDSEY DENNIS
Author, *Buried Dreams: From Devastating Loss to Unimaginable Hope*

Eden Griffith
775-253-9110

KEEPING *the*
FAITH

A STUDY IN JUDE

—

LIANNA DAVIS

MOODY PUBLISHERS

CHICAGO

© 2020 by
LIANNA DAVIS

All rights reserved. No part of this book may be reproduced in any form without permission in writing from the publisher, except in the case of brief quotations embodied in critical articles or reviews.

All Scripture quotations, unless otherwise indicated, are taken from The ESV® Bible (The Holy Bible, English Standard Version®), copyright © 2001 by Crossway, a publishing ministry of Good News Publishers. Used by permission. All rights reserved.

Scripture quotations marked NIV are taken from the Holy Bible, New International Version®, NIV®. Copyright © 1973, 1978, 1984, 2011 by Biblica, Inc.™ Used by permission of Zondervan. All rights reserved worldwide. www.zondervan.com. "NIV" and "New International Version" are trademarks registered in the United States Patent and Trademark Office by Biblica, Inc.™

Scripture quotations marked NASB are taken from the New American Standard Bible® (NASB), Copyright © 1960, 1962, 1963, 1968, 1971, 1972, 1973, 1975, 1977, 1995 by The Lockman Foundation. Used by permission. www.Lockman.org.

Edited by Pamela Joy Pugh
Interior design: Erik M. Peterson
Cover design: Dean Renninger
Cover photo of water colors copyright © 2019 by kostins/Shutterstock (363296042). All rights reserved.

Names: Davis, Lianna B., author.
Title: Keeping the faith : a study in Jude / Lianna B. Davis.
Description: Chicago : Moody Publishers, 2020. | Includes bibliographical
    references. | Summary: "An in-depth, theologically rich study of the
    book of Jude. Learn to treasure the gifts of salvation, the faith, the
    church, and--most of all--Jesus Christ in this new study."-- Provided by publisher.
Identifiers: LCCN 2019030934 (print) | LCCN 2019030935 (ebook) | ISBN
    9780802419316 (paperback) | ISBN 9780802497956 (ebook)
Subjects: LCSH: Bible. Jude--Textbooks.
Classification: LCC BS2815.55 .D38 2020 (print) | LCC BS2815.55 (ebook) |
    DDC 227/.970071--dc23
LC record available at https://lccn.loc.gov/2019030934
LC ebook record available at https://lccn.loc.gov/2019030935

All websites listed herein are accurate at the time of publication but may change in the future or cease to exist. The listing of website references and resources does not imply publisher endorsement of the site's entire contents.

Originally delivered by fleets of horse-drawn wagons, the affordable paperbacks from D. L. Moody's publishing house resourced the church and served everyday people. Now, after more than 125 years of publishing and ministry, Moody Publishers' mission remains the same—even if our delivery systems have changed a bit.

Moody Publishers
820 N. LaSalle Boulevard
Chicago, IL 60610

1 3 5 7 9 10 8 6 4 2

Printed in the United States of America

To my parents, who taught me the faith.

CONTENTS

WHAT TO ANTICIPATE FROM JUDE

The New Testament book of Jude is composed of only twenty-five verses, yet this short epistle is brimming with material that will enrich your understanding of God and draw you closer in your walk with Him in true mercy, peace, and love.

This study is made up of six weeks, with an introduction and five days of lessons for each week. We'll begin with a verse or portion of a verse from Jude, add a pertinent cross reference, and suggest a prayer to introduce thoughts on the day's topic and prompt you to begin your studies before God. Each day's concise sketch on the passage will shed light through examining background, walking through matters of interpretation, and/or considering an application. A series of questions for study and reflection will enhance your understanding and response. You can plan to set aside twenty minutes for each day of study, while having freedom to answer the questions for study and reflection in each day that are most compelling to you personally as you are guided by the Holy Spirit in learning the Word and applying it to your life. This format works well both for individual and group study.

Who is the Jude of our study? His precise identity is rather uncertain and scholars' opinions differ, but we learn a few clues from Scripture. Jude begins his letter by describing himself as a servant of Christ and adds that he's a brother of James. Some identify Jude as the half brother of Jesus (Matt. 13:55; Mark 6:3; see also Gal. 1:19) who possibly served as a missionary and likely a recognized church leader (1 Cor. 9:5).[1] Some suggest he was the apostle Judas (not Iscariot), who was also called Thaddeus (Luke 6:16; Matt. 10:3).[2] Others point out that he does not call himself an apostle.[3] Whatever the case, we do know that he was a respected leader in the church with close apostolic connection and, as we will learn, someone with authority to be heeded.

Throughout this study you will "meet" various commentators, theologians, and pastors whom I have found of immense help and blessing in my studies of Jude.

I find that reading others' words on Scripture does not replace my desire and ability to personally grapple with God's Word before Him. Rather, it provides me a richer, better-guided, and more informed pondering and application of what I read there, spurring me to increasing excellence in my own studies through others' examples. I hope you similarly benefit through this study by our access to the work of many historic and contemporary scholars and teachers who have dedicated themselves to the study of God's Word.

By the end of our six weeks together, you will have a greater biblical knowledge of warnings, false teachers, Enoch, Korah, and others. You will be conversant about theological topics like Gnosticism and antinomianism. You will appreciate Jude's tender heart and "wish-prayer" that encircle his letter. You not only will come to know this brief portion of God's Word very well, but, if you are like me, you will have grown to love it.

Let's get started.

Keeping in Truth

My husband and I were part of a church plant in the beginning of our marriage. One day, before our congregation had a building to call home, we met outside for a baptism service. We, a small, close-knit church body, stood in a semicircle around a backyard lake. To our side, our pastor walked downward, from grass to murk to sandy bottom, accompanying a new believer in Christ.

Professing faith and then being tipped backward into the water, this believer was then launched forward into a life of outward testimony to the risen Christ. We all felt raised in joy alongside this convert. As a small congregation, we had the privilege of pointedly celebrating together each new believer's life, dwelling on the realities of salvation through this unique kind of event. Before our eyes, an inwardly personal decision of faith in Christ was expressed outwardly—our fellow believer was plunged as though into His death and joyous resurrection.

Where death once was, life had come forever. In a town where suburb starts to diverge into rural living, where yards are more expansive and patches of woods surrounded us, our little congregation paused to witness and celebrate spiritual life. These truths bring holy pause to our spirits as believers because they are lofty realities, to be remembered in a world that does not know them, does not know God.

Jude uses the first words of his epistle—after introducing himself—to raise his recipients' heads and hearts to the tremendous realities of salvation: "To those who are called." The epistle of Romans features the same word, "called," twice in

its opening paragraphs, speaking of recipients who are "called to belong to Jesus Christ" and "called to be saints" (Rom. 1:6, 7). This concept has been defined as God's "identification of those whom He names as His own."[1] This call, being named God's own people who are saved out of the world and raised into a position to serve Him in it, informs and directs our days on this earth.

The epistle of Jude, as we study it, will summon our lives forward into more of God's truth. It will inform us about our calling to this position we have gained and help us learn new dimensions of our belonging with Him—soul, spirit, and body.

For the first week, we start with an introduction to Jude's humble, loving, and urgent words to know the truth, to take hold of it and keep it foremost. With Jude's opening words, we pause to remember the implications of our lofty calling.

WEEK 1 | DAY 1

I found it necessary to write appealing to you to contend for the faith that was once for all delivered to the saints.

JUDE 3b

Cross reference: *The aim of our charge is love that issues from a pure heart and a good conscience and a sincere faith.*

1 TIMOTHY 1:5

Father, I thank You for Your Scriptures, which alone are the final, authoritative source of truth. Thank You for the example in Jude of protecting this truth with a heart of sincerity and love.

CONTENDING IS PROTECTING

Recalling the sight of our two-year-old daughter standing on the wrong side of the unlatched baby gate in front of an open, formidable hardwood staircase still makes me cringe. I thank the Lord that shouting her name from the kitchen froze her. Soon, with my arms around a wide-eyed little girl, I had to explain: "You are precious. You mean so very much to me—that is why I had to talk so loudly. Those stairs are dangerous for you, sweetheart. I wanted to keep you from falling!" Before our talk, she only had one side of the story, and I probably sounded short-tempered. But my concern was expressed commensurately with the urgency of the danger and was spoken with a desired effect—to keep my daughter from taking one more step in the wrong direction.

One tone is dominant in the epistle of Jude: forcefulness in defending the church against false teachers within its ranks who are distorting the Christian faith. I also hear the tenderness of Jude's heart, the clarity of his holy understanding of truth, the Christ-keeping-us promise aglow in his concluding thoughts and, most of all, the divine Author superintending his words of love and directness. Jude is not unlike the apostle Paul, who targets false teachers with a "charge" while writing to his protégé Timothy. Paul gives reason behind his words: "The aim of our charge is love that issues from a pure heart and a good conscience and a sincere faith" (1 Tim. 1:5).

At the very start of his letter, Jude hints at why he writes with a sense of urgency, giving early insight into his intentions. Jude's thesis is this: "Beloved, although I was very eager to write to you about our common salvation, I found it necessary to write appealing to you to contend for the faith that was once for all delivered to the saints" (Jude 3).

Being a gospel believer, Jude originally wants to write a letter primarily about the glorious truths of shared salvation—that sin, eternal damnation, and death have been replaced with righteousness, peace in God's eternal presence, and life forevermore through personal faith in Jesus Christ, who died in place of sinners on the cross and rose in victory. But instead, Jude is compelled to communicate: "Warning! Warning! Beloved church, heed my teaching and keep yourselves for Christ—even as He keeps you for Himself." Knowing his forceful words to be warranted, he speaks with genuine concern the most loving words his recipients could have heard in their danger—that contending results in protection of people and preservation of the truth in our contexts. Jude asks his recipients to contend in accordance with their Christ-bought calling, and for the rest of the letter, he shows them how.

For Study *and* Reflection

Read through this letter. Try not to dwell on unfamiliar concepts—Jude writes of such things as the archangel, Korah, Enoch, wandering stars, etc.—but as you read, watch for and then describe Jude's tone. (Remember the toddler near the stairs.)

Jude's overarching theme is to preserve the truth of the faith as established by Christ and passed forward by the apostles. Do you see any repeated words and themes in this book that support that thesis?

Jude will essentially "raise his voice" in the warnings of this letter. As will be evident throughout this coming week of study, Jude writes as one who loves what is worth protecting and preserving. How about you? We live in a cultural context that prizes accommodation to the detriment of conviction. Are you willing to welcome what is convictional—what God asks you to stand for and/or face about yourself?

Jude refers to the lay Christian as a "saint" (v. 3), a holy representative of Christ who has received His truth. How does this description mold your sense of calling in this life?

WEEK 1 | DAY 2

I found it necessary to write appealing to you to contend for the faith that was once for all delivered to the saints.

JUDE 3b

Cross reference: *So then, brothers, stand firm and hold to the traditions that you were taught by us, either by our spoken word or by our letter.*

2 THESSALONIANS 2:15

Father, many in history have risked their livelihoods and reputations, even their very lives, to affirm sound doctrine and pass a right interpretation of who You are along to me. Thank You. Grow in my heart a devotion to You and honor of what You have revealed in Scripture.

DOCTRINE IN RELATIONSHIP

If I did not know that my husband, Tyler, likes technological gadgets, I would not have much inspiration for what he might enjoy as a birthday present. If I didn't know that he would serve other people endlessly, I might never suggest he take some time for himself. If I didn't remember information about his colleagues, responsibilities, and work environment, I wouldn't be able to meaningfully engage in many evening conversations. If I said to Tyler, "I love you so much. But I don't care to know much about you, your interests, your likes and dislikes, or your pursuits," I couldn't really love him very well at all.

I imagine the same kind of disconnect in my relationship with the Lord, were I to think I could love Him without learning and investing myself in what matters to Him—without knowledge of Him, or doctrine. Albert Mohler indicates that doctrinal content plays a crucial role in the evangelical Christian faith:

> There is no faith relation with Christ free of doctrinal content. The knower must have some knowledge of the known, or no relation exists. That seemingly redundant and self-evident statement should underline the issue. Jesus Christ and our knowledge of Him are not in any sense coextensive. But one cannot have a relation with Him without knowledge, and that knowledge represents incipient doctrine.[2]

In day 1, we learned that Jude advocates contending. Contending for what? That's our focus for today. "I found it necessary to write appealing to you to contend for the faith that was once for all delivered to the saints" (v. 3b). "Faith" is used in two ways in the New Testament, "designated by two Latin expressions: *fides quae*, 'the faith that we believe,' and *fides qua*, 'the faith by which we believe.'"[3] In other words, faith is our expression of trust in Christ.

So the faith—*fides quae*—is what we believe in, meaning the doctrinal content. Jude does not need to summarize the body of doctrinal information to which he refers, since at the time of Jude's writing, the "apostolic faith was crystallized (v. 3); the words of the apostles could be recalled (v. 17)."[4] So he assumes his audience's familiarity with it and accountability to it—though some of them are apparently at risk of forgetting. To prevent their drifting, they are to contend, or strive to reverse the current of a lackadaisical attitude toward the faith.

Jude's concern for the faith is an example that has been shared throughout the historic Christian tradition. The great tradition of the Christian faith, with its movements of the Holy Spirit among broad bodies of believers, clarifies human understanding of scriptural doctrine. It seeks to pass forward to future generations a faithful interpretation of Scripture and follows the example of Paul: "So then, brothers, stand firm and *hold to the traditions* that you were taught by us, either by our spoken word or by our letter" (2 Thess. 2:15, emphasis added).

As one example of this kind of tradition, the International Council on Biblical Inerrancy (ICBI) was founded in 1977 in order to defend the precious doctrine of the Scriptures as being without error.[5] This historic council produced "The Chicago Statement on Biblical Inerrancy," which can be found in the appendix. One of the founding members, Jay Grimstead, also helped lead a separate group of theologians and pastors in forming a well-received, transdenominational faith statement, "The 42 Articles on the Essentials of a Christian Worldview."[6] These documents are examples of how prominent believers have contended for truth in our modern-day context, following the admonition of Jude.

While we could easily spend many weeks examining the substance of the faith, I intend to follow Jude's sequence of writing by moving forward with more themes from this epistle in the days ahead. We will briefly touch on doctrinal content in the study questions below.

For Study *and* Reflection

Describe your familiarity with the faith—for example, concerning the nature of the Bible, salvation, God, and mankind.

Read through the statement on biblical inerrancy in the appendix. To similarly review a succinct statement of faith concerning God, the universe, truth, salvation, and more, you can link to "The 42 Articles on the Essentials of a Christian Worldview" via my website: **www.liannabdavis.com/faith-statement**. Record what is especially new to you. Feel free to note any questions that come to mind as points for further personal study.

What is your reaction to the quote from Al Mohler and to the extent of Jude's concern for the faith?

What does Mohler imply about how Christians grow closer with Christ? Does this affect the way you think about growing closer with Christ?

Does doctrine seem to be life-giving, dry, or something in between? Are your feelings about doctrine compatible with the scriptural example of believers who have given of themselves for this work of contending?

WEEK 1 | DAY 3

*Jude, a servant of Jesus Christ and brother of
James . . .*
JUDE 1a

Cross reference: *But thanks be to God, that you who were once slaves of sin
have become obedient from the heart to the standard of teaching to which
you were committed.*
ROMANS 6:17

*Father, I see that the opposite of being a slave to sin is a life obedient to the standard of
teaching You have put forward in the Scriptures as being a joyful, willing slave to You.
My life belongs to You.*

A HUMBLE REPRESENTATIVE

Thinking ahead to the ungodly, selfish ways of the false teachers exposed later in
Jude's epistle—which you likely observed in your initial reading—Jude's example
of godly leadership is a clear, refreshing juxtaposition: he is desirous of being a
humble servant, is well-qualified for his endeavors, and is devoted to the truth.

Jude describes himself in verse 1 as, "Jude, a servant of Jesus Christ." Now turn to Romans 6:16–18. From these verses in Romans, we can note that being a servant of Jesus Christ—also translated "bondslave" (Greek *doulos*)—is true of all born-again Christians. All mankind has only two options, two types of possible slavery—slavery to sin and death or slavery to Christ.

First, being Christ's is the great result of salvation. Because we are in Christ, having become God's own with our whole lives, present and future, we can joyously consider the connotations of being a slave of Christ: "pertaining to a state of being completely controlled by someone or something—'subservient to, controlled by.'"[7] Believers are not only released from sin, but set in the safe and utter belonging of God.

Second, a servant, or bondslave, of Jesus Christ is also a specific title in Scripture used to describe someone "who is charged to labour in Christ's service" as an "authorized . . . representative."[8] This specialized meaning is true in both the Old and New Testaments (see, for example, Josh. 14:7; 2 Kings 17:23; Ps. 89:3, 20; Rom. 1:1; Gal. 1:10; Phil. 1:1; Col. 4:12; Titus 1:1; James 1:1; 2 Peter 1:1).

Referring to himself as a servant, or bondslave, in his introduction, "the implication is, not simply that Jude is a Christian but that he is a recognized leader with a claim to speak and be listened to."[9] When Paul writes to Timothy, he warns of false teachers: "They want to be teachers of the law, but they do not know what they are talking about or what they so confidently affirm" (1 Tim. 1:7 NIV). By contrast, Jude is an approved leader; he diligently handles God's revelation (cf. 2 Tim. 2:15).

For Study *and* Reflection

Do you see yourself as having ownership over yourself? What does it mean to welcome the ownership of someone else? (See Gal. 2:20.)

Why is Jesus Christ deserving of this ownership? (Refer to Col. 1:18 and Eph. 1:20–22.)

How does Romans 6:16–18 describe the joys of being a bondslave of Christ?

Jude is an authorized representative (i.e., trained and commissioned by church leadership) of doctrine. As a lay Christian, how can you honor the value of biblical expertise and of trained Christian leaders? (See 1 Thess. 5:12–13.)

WEEK 1 | DAY 4

Beloved, although I was very eager to write to you about our common salvation, I found it necessary to write appealing to you . . .

JUDE 3a; cf. JUDE 1a

Cross reference: *Simeon Peter, a servant and apostle of Jesus Christ, To those who have obtained a faith of equal standing with ours by the righteousness of our God and Savior Jesus Christ . . .*

2 PETER 1:1

Father, thank You that I have access to Your truth. It was not merely given to a private group of Your followers but delivered to the whole of us. Thank You that You desire to be known by Your people and that we share in You together.

LEADING FROM THE TRUTH

While Jude's letter is on the topic of contending for the faith against false teachers, Jude originally desires to compose his letter about general, joyous themes of salvation in Christ, which he and his letter's recipients share in common. This salvation of Christ is shared among all believers (see Eph. 4:5–6), and Paul summarizes this message when writing to those at Corinth:

For I delivered to you as of first importance what I also received: that Christ died for our sins in accordance with the Scriptures, that he was buried, that he was raised on the third day in accordance with the Scriptures, and that he appeared to Cephas, then to the twelve.
—1 Corinthians 15:3–5

Though Jude desires to dwell on these themes, he changes direction because a specific situation has come to his attention (see vv. 3–4). According to authors David J. Hesselgrave and Ronald P. Hesselgrave, Jude's original desire in writing his letter is instructive.

> Only those who desire to major on God's "so great salvation" are justified in dwelling upon the erroneous teachings, attitudes, and actions that abrogate it. If a teacher becomes wholly preoccupied with error in the Church, there is a strong likelihood that his spirit will become sour, critical, and abrasive. . . . It is the teacher who wants to major on salvation who is best qualified to warn against error because, inevitably, he will do it with compassion in his heart, a tear in his eye, and compulsion in his voice.[10]

Because of Jude's love for his letter's recipients and his joy in the salvation of Christ, he changes the content of his letter to that of a warning. This desire to warn and instruct for the good of others when their reactions to warning are unknown is a mark of a leader. Jude does not list all his qualifications in this letter. He gives validity to the letter through the prominence of James, likely referring to the disciple/apostle (Matt. 17:1; Gal. 2:9) and pillar of the Jerusalem church who was Jesus' half brother (Acts 15:13–21; 21:18; Gal. 1:19). Jude seems to avoid being presumptuous with his qualifications out of a desire to draw attention to the message of his letter; its recipients were to heed his words not simply because of Jude's personal stature, but because the truth he writes matters to the Lord, and thus, to both writer and recipients through Him.

FOR STUDY *and* REFLECTION

Consider that Jude is not parading his qualifications and originally desires to write about the shared message of salvation. What do these characteristics communicate about his priorities and the genuineness of his concerns? What Christian leadership qualities does he embody? Refer to Mark 10:42–45; 1 Peter 5:3; Philippians 2:3–8; and 1 Timothy 4:16.

Jude's lack of pointed appeal to his own qualifications does not mean he writes with any less certainty about the message of his letter. What is the basis for the certainty of his message? See Ephesians 2:20 and 1 Corinthians 3:11.

Look back to the questions of day 1 to remember the tone of Jude's letter. As you consider the humility of Jude and his leadership qualities when introducing himself, do you have any different impressions about the tone of the letter now?

How might Jude's intentions help you evaluate your motivations prior to correcting someone else or standing for truth against false teaching?

Jude, a trained and commissioned leader, points away from himself to Jesus Christ and to the authority of another. How can you follow his model? Give an example.

WEEK 1 | DAY 5

To those who are called, beloved in God the Father and kept for Jesus Christ . . .

JUDE 1B

"And Can It Be, That I Should Gain?" by Charles Wesley

And can it be that I should gain
An int'rest in the Savior's blood?
Died He for me, who caused His pain?
For me, who Him to death pursued?
Amazing love! how can it be
That Thou, my God, should die for me?

'Tis mystery all! Th'Immortal dies!
Who can explore His strange design?
In vain the firstborn seraph tries
To sound the depths of love divine!
'Tis mercy all! let earth adore,
Let angel minds inquire no more.

He left His Father's throne above,
So free, so infinite His grace;
Emptied Himself of all but love,
And bled for Adam's helpless race;
'Tis mercy all, immense and free;
For, O my God, it found out me.

Long my imprisoned spirit lay
Fast bound in sin and nature's night;
Thine eye diffused a quick'ning ray,
I woke, the dungeon flamed with light;
My chains fell off, my heart was free;
I rose, went forth and followed Thee.

No condemnation now I dread;
Jesus, and all in Him is mine!
Alive in Him, my living Head,
And clothed in righteousness divine,
Bold I approach th'eternal throne,
And claim the crown, through Christ
    my own.

Refrain:
Amazing love! how can it be
That Thou, my God, should die for me![11]

KEPT IN LOVE

For a brief letter replete with warnings, Jude manages to frequently remind his recipients of their status as God's beloved (see vv. 1, 3, 17, and 20). The love of Christ is in view. Now, Jude's letter warns about those who are doctrinally in error—perhaps some who are genuine believers sorrowfully swayed by falsehood and some who have never been genuine believers. But Jude writes not directly to this group that is in error but about them. He writes to the church, with the implication that all believers stand to benefit from reading of God's warnings of destruction for those who are unbelieving.

Perhaps this is why Jude reminds his recipients of God's love. Without it in view, a genuine believer may be tempted to dismiss God's warnings, believing she is above and/or beyond needing them as a recipient of grace. Or, she may worry that if these warnings do have application to her, then she is not really who she thinks she is—perhaps not a true believer after all.

If you and I fear the truth about ourselves, perhaps we are worried that Christ's love will disappear when all is revealed about how needy we are, failing to recognize the grace that Christ's love is received by those who are, by definition, poor and lost. Or if we view Scripture's warnings as unnecessary, perhaps we are slow to recognize the gravity of sin, diminishing our hatred for why our precious Lord died. Or perhaps we are not recognizing that Christ has come to form us into who we could never be without His love—people with increasing longing for holiness. Or, perhaps some of us have not exposed ourselves to the warnings of Scripture very much at all.

Whatever our reactions to the warnings of Scripture, we do well to calibrate our hearts to be receptive to them. In Christ's love, the necessary punishment for the believer's sin has been lifted. Not fearing the punishment of God is the very freedom that leads us to be perfected, or sanctified. It gives the security and confidence that is needed to openly acknowledge sins so that they can be confessed and abandoned. And contemplating the extent of Christ's sacrificial and suffering love helps us to increasingly hate sin. Reminded of being beloved by God, we are given all the reason, soberness, and security we need to take Jude's warnings to heart.

The warnings of God benefit the beloved of God; these warnings function to keep us near to God's heart in a world filled with messages that oppose the truth. "Kept" is how Jude addresses his believing recipients in verse 1 immediately after calling them "beloved." Jude does not invent this concept of God's loving keeping. Jesus prays, for example, for the safe keeping of His own in the High Priestly Prayer of John 17:8–19. He outlines a pattern of security in this world for the people of God. No longer slaves to sin, believers are those not of the world because they have inwardly received the Word from heaven (vv. 8, 14). Having received the Word of heaven they are brought nearer to heavenly ways and are made saintlier in the truth (v. 17). Being made more heavenly, they can further partake of the character of divine love, which is true and holy (v. 26).

As our study in Jude progresses, we can take heart that receiving the truth of God's love in Christ is how we are freed to receive difficult truths with confidence and, in heeding these difficult truths, we become freed of sin and falsehood, able to fellowship in a more heavenly way with Christ in us, in purer love.

For Study *and* Reflection

Read John 8:31–38 and John 17:26. Describe how God's words being in us and Christ being in us are related.

How does Jude's purpose statement (see days 1 and 2) issue from the very desires of the Lord in John 17:8–19? Do you see any ways in which Jude's thesis is an answer to the Lord's prayer in John? Explain.

As is clear from an introductory reading of Jude, warnings are ahead in this study. What is your heart's reaction to scriptural warnings of judgment for sin? Do we experience fear that who we really are will be exposed through Scripture's warnings? Are we tempted to dismiss the warnings of Scripture as unneeded because "I am saved"?

According to Jude 21, to what do warnings lead us? According to Jude 24–25, what is our heart's response after we have received biblical warnings as intended?

How does this encourage you to welcome Jude's warnings ahead?

Reread the words to "And Can It Be, That I Should Gain?" or listen to a recording of this great hymn. What gospel truths communicated in this hymn nourish your spirit today as God's beloved?

Keeping in Grace

I joke with my husband that one of the reasons for the strength of our relationship is, well, his memory. Don't misunderstand—as an actuary, he analyzes complicated mathematical formulas daily. So I am convinced that while he could remember my offenses toward him, he chooses and somehow manages to not remember them. When I sit down with Tyler to describe how my end of a conversation had been plaguing my conscience, I tell him, for example, what I did, what tone I used, or what inadequacy on his part I inaccurately implied—and he typically replies, "You did? Thanks for telling me, but I don't remember." In my relationship with him, I directly experience God's mercy of remembering our sins no more!

When I was younger and allowed a classmate who had not studied to cheat by copying from my test, I came home to my parents crushed. When I confessed and asked what my punishment would be, they mercifully said, "You have punished yourself enough." When I replied that I had asked God over and over to please forgive me, they gently told me that one time of genuinely and repentantly asking His forgiveness was enough. In both of these situations, I did not receive the punishment I was due—but received mercy in response to acknowledgment of my offense. These remain examples to me of the Lord's graciousness.

We must note that Jude's letter is not directed toward believers who are recognizing sins in their lives and tenderheartedly confessing them. Jude's concern is of a different nature: a church has allowed unbiblical teachings to seep within and sway believers and would-be believers without any confrontation, care, or negation!

The very context that should serve as a pillar and buttress of truth (1 Tim. 3:15) is leading people away from God with its bleak confusions. Consequences are dire. Jude frequents themes of warning concerning condemnation (v. 4), destruction (v. 5), God's judgment (vv. 6, 15), punishment of eternal fire (v. 7), pronouncement of woe (v. 11), perishing (v. 11), gloom of utter darkness (v. 13; cf. 6), conviction (v. 15), and fire (v. 23).

Jude cannot focus his letter primarily on the characteristics and truths of God's mercy, as his readers would be oblivious to the need in their circumstance without first being warned! The only way to lead them to mercy would be to remind them of destruction and alert them about their dangerous related steps. Jude does desire his recipients to know mercy—in the vein my parents and husband have demonstrated to me.

Mercy, peace, and love (v. 2), three facets of God's grace, are not removed from Jude's purpose; he progresses to these themes (vv. 21–23) through the necessary avenue of warning.

WEEK 2 | DAY 1

For certain people have crept in unnoticed . . .
JUDE 4a

Cross reference: Beware of false prophets, who come to you in sheep's
clothing but inwardly are ravenous wolves.
MATTHEW 7:15

---

*Father, I thank You for sending me the strong warnings of Scripture by which I can more
clearly understand Your teachings. These warnings are forceful, bold, and true—not
brash, regretted, or unnecessarily employed. You are deliberate, piercingly wise, and accurate in Your revelation.*

FORCEFUL WORDS OF GENTLENESS

Can a believer be both derogatory and gentle? These may not seem complementary
at first glance, but we might need more than a first glance. In *Exegetical Fallacies*,
D. A. Carson warns against false disjunctions. We create false disjunctions when
an "either/or" mentality is falsely assumed in reading the Bible, leading to error in
interpretation, e.g., "Either gentleness is right or being derogatory is right—but it
cannot be both!"[1] Instead, he recommends considering how two biblical teachings

might complement each other. A false disjunction might be assumed between gentleness and the style of language Jude uses when discussing the false teachers:

> Jude described them as "certain men," which many commentators feel is a slightly disparaging reference to the interlopers. The verbal form used of the opponents (they "have secretly slipped in") is certainly derogatory.[2]

But many areas of Scripture use similar—or stronger!—language concerning any who tamper with the truth. Consider the following verses.

> John: "If anyone comes to you and does not bring this teaching, do not receive him into your house or give him any greeting." (2 John 1:10)

> Paul: "Wake up from your drunken stupor . . ." (1 Cor. 15:34a)

> Paul: "But even if we or an angel from heaven should preach to you a gospel contrary to the one we preached to you, let him be accursed." (Gal. 1:8)

> Paul: "Look out for the dogs, look out for the evildoers . . ." (Phil. 3:2)

> Jesus: "Beware of false prophets, who come to you in sheep's clothing but inwardly are ravenous wolves." (Matt. 7:15)

> Jesus: "You serpents, you brood of vipers, how are you to escape being sentenced to hell?" (Matt. 23:33)

The church fathers continued in the tradition of using this language. To the Ephesians, Ignatius (c. 25–107), the bishop of Antioch in Syria, wrote:

> For there are some who are accustomed to carrying about the Name maliciously and deceitfully while doing other things unworthy of God. You must avoid them as wild beasts. For they are mad dogs that bite by stealth; you must be on your guard against them, for their bite is hard to heal.[3]

Having listed various examples of forceful, derogatory language, let us also consider a biblical concept of gentleness. Paul, when requiring the church at Corinth to listen to his corrections, says that he "[entreats] by the meekness and gentleness of Christ" (2 Cor. 10:1). The Greek term for gentleness here is *epieikeia*, which "suggests the yielding of a judge, who, instead of demanding the exact penalty required by strict justice, gives way to circumstances which call for mercy."[4]

I think of how God did not exact the fullness of the punishment for sin in the garden of Eden by sending Adam and Eve immediately to hell. He would have been just to do so but chose to demonstrate His gentleness and mercy by making a future way for Christ's salvation.

Therefore, to learn from Paul about communicating truth in the gentleness of Christ, derisive language is to be used as Jude does: to clearly delineate truth from falsehood so that hearers know how to be restored to the Lord in His mercy. Leading others toward God's mercy certainly does not always require such language, as I have often experienced! But in Jude's context it was required; it is included within his complete framework of instructions that involves restoring those in the church to truth and having mercy on those who doubt and fear (see Jude 23–24).

This is at least one way the two—derogatory language and gentleness—are complementary: Jude's language has the grit to communicate that God's eternal truth can never compromise with the world and the force to fittingly and accurately alert others to the need for God's mercy. For, first, a gentle person remembers his or her dependence on God's grace. Second, toward God's grace the gentle person intends to lead others so that, prayerfully, truth will no longer need to come in the form of a warning but can be cherished together.

For Study *and* Reflection

Revisit the examples of strong language from Scripture and church history, and consider what this language accomplishes—it is not used without purpose. What is communicated about false teachers in each of these examples, and in what ways are the various analogies profitable? What did the reader not know about the false teachers or teaching that they come to know through them?

Read Jude again. What does Jude's forceful and derogatory language accomplish?

Read 2 Timothy 2:24–26, 2 Corinthians 10:1, and Philippians 1:27–28. What do you learn about biblical contending?

Have you ever experienced words forceful in truth that led you toward God's mercy? If so, describe. Perhaps you have experienced the opposite: Words forceful in truth did not ever carry the intention of directing you to God's mercy in Christ. If so, with Paul's words in mind, what might you do or say differently than what you have experienced?

WEEK 2 | DAY 2

For certain people have crept in unnoticed . . .
JUDE 4a

Now I want to remind you, although you once fully knew it . . .
JUDE 5

Cross reference: *For the time is coming when people will not endure sound teaching, but having itching ears they will accumulate for themselves teachers to suit their own passions, and will turn away from listening to the truth and wander off into myths.*
2 TIMOTHY 4:3–4

Father, I want the fullness of Your Word to rule my inner being—make me receptive to all You have to teach me, and let me choose teachers who have the same desire.

KEPT BY REMINDERS AND WARNINGS

"Blessed is the man who walks not in the counsel of the wicked, nor stands in the way of sinners, nor sits in the seat of scoffers." Psalm 1:1 shows a progression for falling away from the truth of Scripture: *walking* with wicked counsel, *standing* in the way of this counsel, and then openly *sitting* in congruence with evil. Reformer John Calvin writes that this verse "shows how, by little and little, men are ordinarily induced to turn aside from the right path. They do not, at the first step, advance so far as a proud contempt of God, but having once begun to give ear to evil counsel, Satan leads them, step by step, farther astray, till they rush headlong into open transgression."[5]

Second Timothy 4:3–4 reveals a similar pattern: *listening* to instruction that is not sound, taking action by *turning* from truth, and, finally, *wandering* off altogether. Both patterns begin with listening. Those who do not carefully listen to what is influencing them, comparing what they hear against Scripture, are considered unwary by church father Irenaeus (c. 130–202) as he discusses how people are led astray:

> Error, indeed, is never set forth in its naked deformity, lest, being thus exposed, it should at once be detected. But it is craftily decked out in an attractive dress, so as, by its outward form, to make it appear to the inexperienced . . . more true than the truth itself.[6]

We might grow comfortable with our patterns of thinking, even when falsehood is slyly interwoven, because either the world or the Christian cultural context in which we find ourselves has made our hearing dull. We might not be aware of the errors of thinking to which we adhere; that is the very background of Jude's word in verse 4. John MacArthur explains it this way:

> The word translated **crept in unnoticed** (*pareisduō*) appears only here in the New Testament. It has the connotation of slipping in secretly with an evil intention. In extrabiblical Greek it described the cunning craftiness of a lawyer who, through clever argumentation, infiltrated the minds of courtroom officials and corrupted their thinking. Having already permeated the church, the apostates were in position to "secretly introduce destructive heresies." (2 Peter 2:1)[7]

Detecting error can be a challenge; it can creep in unobserved. Therefore, we can learn to have an attitude of receptivity and genuine consideration toward the reminders and warnings of other believers—even if our first natural reaction is dismissal of these. Thankfully, we have each other, in the local church and broader church, to alert us and help our faith be preserved.

FOR STUDY *and* REFLECTION

According to Proverbs 12:15, in what ways do the foolish and the wise differ? What is indicated here, and in similar proverbs, about being receptive to warnings?

Consider the overall pattern of falling away from the truth taught in Psalm 1 and 2 Timothy 4:3–4. Do you find yourself edging toward any stage in that sequence? In what way(s) can you be helped by others to detect your patterns, and in what way(s) is this discernment a personal responsibility that you cannot necessarily rely on others to do for you?

When is the last time you tested what you heard against the truth? What was the result of your findings? (Some ways you can do this include researching the background of a teacher to discern his or her influences; searching reviews of a book that compare its contents with Scripture; or initiating a personal study of Scripture on a topic in question. Can you think of others?)

Ponder these questions:

When you do notice an error in your understanding, do you ever excuse it or dismiss it as insignificant?

Are you tempted to believe that because others clearly hold to the same error, turning from it may be unimportant?

Or are you resolved to turn from any and every unscriptural error because the truth of Scripture is not to be compromised?

In what way(s) do you consistently walk in the direction of biblical truth and counsel, examining the messages you hear and believe, and in what ways would you like to grow in doing so?

WEEK 2 | DAY 3

. . . who long ago were designated for this condemnation . . .

JUDE 4b

Cross reference: *Now the Spirit expressly says that in later times some will depart from the faith by devoting themselves to deceitful spirits and teachings of demons . . .*

1 TIMOTHY 4:1

Father, I know that You have determined to punish evil; by Your grace, I devote myself to what is good.

THE END OF FALSE TEACHERS

The church members to whom Jude writes and the false teachers Jude has in mind are, at the time of Jude's composition, enjoying each other in the context of the church, feasting together (v. 12). Jude is calling the true believers to reject those who do not hold to true doctrine—on an initial reading, the request seems straightforward. But on a personal level, bonds have surely been formed. These undetected false teachers are people with whom the true believers have strong, enjoyable memories, mingled with their most intimate experiences of church. So

Jude carefully clarifies that he does not merely have a personal vendetta against the false teachers—this is not a clash of personalities.

Jude writes God-breathed words on His authority, so the recipients can know that if they fail to reject the unrepentant false teachers, the recipients will not simply be failing Jude—but failing God. Surely, Jude's words were met with an element of surprise. But, comfort of all comforts, God was certainly not taken by surprise by the false teachers.

According to Proverbs 16:4, "The LORD has made everything for its purpose, even the wicked for the day of trouble." Classic commentator Matthew Henry explains: "He makes no man wicked, but he made those who he foresaw would be wicked,"[8] and another scholar tells us that "the judgment in Jude, then, refers to the judgment that was foreseen by God."[9]

God knew that such false teachers would penetrate the church, be unrepentant, and continue to the end on a path of destruction—certain destruction because God has consistently worked in history to judge sin. Based on the foreknowledge and character of God, therefore, Jude can write that the false teachers were designated, or "'prescripted' (*progegrammenoi*) long ago," to condemnation.[10] Jude, seemingly, anticipates at the opening of his letter the condemning words that are coming and interjects this assurance from the foreknowledge and character of God to encourage his recipients to cling to the truth even when interpersonal relationships have been formed.

The end of these once-comrades of the church who do not repent is sorrowfully dire; what the unrepentant will meet in the end is unalterable, despite how pleasant shared experiences have seemed.

FOR STUDY *and* REFLECTION

Read Philippians 2:12. How does a consideration of condemnation for the ungodly help us value and commit to sound doctrine?

Jude suggests later that people can be pulled out of the fire of condemnation (v. 23). Even Jude is not aware who will ultimately repent and be saved—he simply knows that God has prescribed condemnation for the unrepentant. How does Jude's example encourage us to view speaking truth as compassionate?

Read Romans 2:1–4 and Luke 6:37 and respond to the following:

Who is "elevated" over others in sinful judgment of people by people?

Whom does Jude seek to elevate with his words?

Why is Jude not guilty of violating Romans 2:1–4 and Luke 6:37?

Read Proverbs 17:15 and 1 Corinthians 5:12–13. Why would it be an abomination to the Lord for true believing recipients of Jude's letter to ignore it and take no action as a church?

Charles Hodge writes: "To condemn is to pronounce guilty; or worthy of punishment. To justify is to declare not guilty; or that justice does not demand punishment; or that the person concerned cannot justly be condemned."[11] Read Romans 5:18, 8:1 and 8:33–34. We become among those who are *not* condemned—but justified by grace—through putting our faith in Jesus. Why must being pronounced not guilty lead our beliefs and behaviors in the opposite direction of the false teachers? (See Jude 4b and 1 Timothy 4:1 for the direction of false teachers.)

Reflect: Are you encouraged that people can change in response to hearing the truth? Who can you think of who has experienced such a change?

. . . ungodly people, who pervert the grace of our God into sensuality and deny our only Master and Lord, Jesus Christ . . .

JUDE 4

Cross reference: *For we did not follow cleverly devised myths when we made known to you the power and coming of our Lord Jesus Christ, but we were eyewitnesses of his majesty.*

2 PETER 1:16

Father, thank You for the testimony of those who have come before me to the truth of who the Lord Jesus Christ is and what He came on this earth to do. If there is a twisting of Your grace within my thoughts, attitudes, or actions, please show it to me so that I can confess and follow You—not merely man.

RIGHT BELIEF AND RIGHT BEHAVIOR

The precise identity of the false teachers to whom Jude refers is elusive. In verse 12, he calls them "shepherds feeding themselves." Various commentaries[12] concur that no conclusive identifying evidence exists. However, some scholars at various times in church history have suggested that similarities exist between the beginnings of Gnosticism and the errors about which Jude writes. The dating for Jude's epistle is typically placed within the second half of the first century, and by that time, early Gnostic influences (called protognosticism) were present.

Some of the tenets of the Gnostic movement are as follows. Instead of a once-for-all delivered faith concerning salvation from sin and judgment, these Gnostics promoted some sort of secret knowledge as the basis of salvation (little is known about this secret knowledge because of how, well, secretive these groups were in their writings). Salvation was considered release from the physical world, which is a mistaken world. Instead of Christ taking on human flesh and nature, Christ is merely like an angelic messenger—only *seeming* to have a physical body—who has "come to earth in order to remind us of our heavenly origin and to give us the secret knowledge without which we cannot return to the spiritual mansions [of the Gnostics' myths]."[13] Some Gnostics further disregarded the physical, believing that "what we are to do is to leave the body to its own devices and let it follow the guidance of its own passions."[14]

This all could potentially correspond to much of what Jude is compelled to write: that the faith has been delivered to all (v. 3), rather than to some in possession of secret knowledge; that Jesus is Lord and Master (v. 4), rather than messenger; and that the interlopers are dreamers (perhaps of Gnostic myths) defiling flesh when without restraint (v. 8). However, parallels with all areas of Gnostic teaching are not present in Jude. (For example, Jude does not discuss false teachers as believing matter to be evil and the created world being a mistaken one that traps human beings in bodies.) Therefore, any potential Gnostic references in Jude would be to an early form. This study will not adhere to any particular identity (Gnostic or otherwise) of the false teachers as an interpretive guide.

Yet, I find considering the possibility of Gnostic influences in Jude's opponents helpful as an example of how an underlying belief system could have influenced the interlopers' behavior. Gnostics had an understanding of Christ and resulting way of living in the flesh that distorted the truth; therefore, Gnostics followed a loose, ungodly lifestyle.[15] Whatever the false teachers' system of belief, it was used to rationalize their behavior, presumably causing the church members under their influence to excuse or not notice their lifestyle—perhaps they were deceived themselves or they were concerned but also did not know how to negate the false teachers' thoughts. Though God has not revealed to us a precise historical identity of these false teachers, Jude's point is clear: wrong beliefs lead to wrong behavior (cf. Jude 3).

I once had a heart-to-heart conversation with a relatively new professing believer, and in the course of our talk, we broached the subject of a certain behavior of hers she was already aware I did not condone. I sought to tell her why wanting to honor the Lord had led me in a different direction with regard to that matter. She replied with something like: "In my walk with the Lord, I have not been convicted about that." To her, the conversation was complete, without any need or desire to discuss the matter further. I was surprised in the moment and felt lost about what to say next. In hindsight I can discern that, beyond behavior, her underlying belief about Scripture was at issue.

Her beliefs about the Christian way of living were based on subjective feelings of her "experience" with God, not on the objective revelation in Scripture of God's holy will having its "sway in the inward parts."[16] It may have been due to her being a fairly new believer, but her feelings of God were her authority, and I could have opened a conversation with her about this. Instead, I remained focused on the behavior, making the error that Douglas Moo writes of in his commentary on Jude: "We are narrowly practical in our focus, myopically concentrating on the 'bottom line' of behavior to the exclusion of everything else."[17]

When my friend and I disagreed on behavior, I did not know where to turn. I did not think to discuss objective biblical beliefs—like the nature of Scripture and its role in the Christian life—as Jude wisely pleads for his recipients to consider.

FOR STUDY *and* REFLECTION

Review the appendix and, if applicable, review from week 1 what you learned through "The 42 Articles on the Essentials of a Christian Worldview." Previously, you were asked to give special attention to any areas that were new. Now, reflect on whether or not these truths are your own, rooted and planted within you. Does Scripture have ultimate sway in your inward parts?

When a specific behavior in your life needs to change, why might ignoring inner change of belief be counterproductive? (Remember the new believer who did not feel convicted about unbiblical behavior.)

According to the example passages below, what are some ways Scripture changes us inwardly—not simply behaviorally?

Applications of Truth to the Inner Person

PASSAGE	INWARD TRANSFORMATION
"God is spirit, and those who worship him must worship in spirit and truth" (John 4:24).	
"Do not be conformed to this world, but be transformed by the renewal of your mind, that by testing you may discern what is the will of God, what is good and acceptable and perfect" (Rom. 12:2).	
"Finally, brothers, whatever is true, whatever is honorable, whatever is just, whatever is pure, whatever is lovely, whatever is commendable, if there is any excellence, if there is anything worthy of praise, think about these things" (Phil. 4:8).	
"You shall love the Lord your God with all your heart and with all your soul and with all your might" (Deut. 6:5).	
"Create in me a clean heart, O God, and renew a right spirit within me" (Ps. 51:10).	
"Oh how I love your law! It is my meditation all the day" (Ps. 119:97).	
"Do not love the world or the things in the world. If anyone loves the world, the love of the Father is not in him" (1 John 2:15).	
"Humble yourselves, therefore, under the mighty hand of God so that at the proper time he may exalt you, casting all your anxieties on him, because he cares for you" (1 Peter 5:6–7).	

First Peter 1:15 teaches: "be holy in all your conduct." According to 1 Peter 1:13, 18–19, what joyous hope and knowledge ultimately propel our conduct to change, as we believe?

WEEK 2 | DAY 5

May mercy, peace, and love be multiplied to you.
JUDE 2

For certain people . . . ungodly people, who pervert the grace of our God into sensuality and deny our only Master and Lord, Jesus Christ.
JUDE 4

"Lord, Keep Us Steadfast in Thy Word" *by Martin Luther*

Lord, keep us steadfast in your Word;
curb those who by deceit or sword
would wrest the kingdom from your Son
and bring to naught all he has done.

Lord Jesus Christ, your pow'r make known,
For you are Lord of lords alone;

defend your holy church, that we
may sing your praise triumphantly.

O Comforter of priceless worth,
send peace and unity on earth;
support us in our final strife,
and lead us out of death to life.[18]

JUDE'S WISH-PRAYER

Jude's type of greeting in verse 2—"May mercy, peace, and love be multiplied to you"—was a standard in letter-writing of his day. But for the biblical writers, these greetings are modified: "In Christian hands, the stereotypical greeting and wish for health become wish-prayers offered to God, which entreat him to grant the recipients the fundamental blessings of the gospel."[19] By his use of "multiplied," Jude's wish-prayer for his recipients is that they would experience these elements of God's grace—mercy, peace, and love—in increasing measure.[20]

Jude's greeting is further unique—different from those in all other New Testament epistles. It is the only one that omits the word grace (with the exception of James's epistle, in which a simple "Greetings" is given in James 1:1), and the only one that includes love. Including *grace* in a greeting at the time was so common that Jude's exclusion of the word in his greeting is noteworthy. This is not to say that Jude strikes grace in favor of other concepts for his opening. But evidently, Jude imports special content and thoughtfulness into this greeting. This prepares his readers for his writing ahead: the triad of mercy, peace, and love are concepts "woven into the fabric of his epistle and, therefore, this wish-prayer serves as an introduction to the fundamental themes he will take up."[21]

Jude's letter was, in effect, going to multiply to his recipients a doctrine of gospel grace, threefold. While the false teachers were distorting grace, Jude would be multiplying true grace in their midst through his truth-filled clarifications. In wanting to write about "common salvation" (v. 3) he likely wanted to write words that would be easily received in immediate, mutual joy. But instead, his letter must convey warnings since the false teachers among his recipients had not yet been denounced. As the recipients are corrected and perceive the truth clearly, Jude extends his great hope from the onset that his readers would receive his words well and be able to, in the end, rejoice that they have come to refine their comprehension of grace in Jesus Christ—in its mercy, peace, and love.

Now, in verse 4, Jude introduces another triad—three characteristics of the false teachers: "First, they are godless (*asebeia*). Second, they change God's grace into a license for immorality (*aselgeia*). Third, they are guilty of lawlessness (*anomia*)."[22]

During weeks 3 through 5 of this study, we will explore how Jude's gospel clarifications provide an abundant understanding of mercy instead of lawlessness, of peace instead of irreverence, and love instead of licentiousness. While I do not pretend to know that these are the specific connotations Jude had in mind, I do observe this opportunity to study the mercy, peace, and love of God in a way that corresponds with Jude's primary themes—in a way that fits within the spirit of his overarching wish-prayer for those who would read his words.

Instead of being those who "deny our only Master and Lord, Jesus Christ," we can grow through considerations ahead to know and worship Him better. As Luther writes in "Lord, Keep Us Steadfast in Thy Word" above—we worship by highly honoring what Christ has done on the cross, regarding Him alone as Lord, and praising Him as the One of priceless worth.

For Study *and* Reflection

When you hear of someone distorting the faith, what is the impulse of your heart? Do you think, *Oh, I wish this person really knew the gospel!* and, if applicable, *Do I have a role in helping to lift this person to know the truth of God's gospel?* Or are you ever tempted to disparage this person rather than hope he or she will be reached with the truth?

Read the book of Jude again. Days 1, 2, and 3 of this week of study examined three intertwined ways Jude will help keep us in the truth: his derogatory language, his reminders and warnings, and his pronouncements of condemnation. What do these aspects of Jude's letter tell us about God's character? What is gracious about these aspects of Jude's letter?

How can you anticipate you will be nourished by the purity, straightness, and narrowness of Jude's words?

We will be studying the following words further as we progress, but for now, briefly jot down your understanding of:

Christ's mercy

His peace

His love

Refer to "Lord, Keep Us Steadfast in Thy Word" by the reformer Martin Luther above. In his wise understanding of doctrinal conflict, what does Luther help us understand is at stake when doctrine is compromised?

How does this hymn help you note the importance of Jude's letter?

Keeping the Soul

"Wild waves of the sea, casting up the foam of their own shame" (v.13a) is Jude's description of the false teachers who are misleading the church he addresses. Isaiah 57:20 is a helpful cross reference to further describe the wildness of the wicked: "But the wicked are like the tossing sea; for it cannot be quiet, and its waters toss up mire and dirt."

How different from godly leaders in Scripture, like King Josiah! Almost like a long-forgotten treasure, the Book of the Law was rediscovered under this king's rule (2 Kings 22:8). In his power, he did not cause others to receive the mire and dirt tossed up by the kind of man who rejects the Book in order to follow his own heart (Isa. 57:17, 20). Rather, King Josiah "tore his clothes" in contrition on his first hearing (2 Kings 22:11) of God's law. He looked to the God who "revive[s] the spirit of the lowly, and . . . the heart of the contrite" (Isa. 57:15). In his position of power, Josiah brought himself humbly before the Lord in private and then cast forward a vision for his people of returning to God.

With this king who "did what was right in the eyes of the Lord" (2 Kings 22:2), power bowed before it led. In addition to his contrition at the Book of the Law being read by those under his supervision, he also could accept correction from godly counselors. One of these biblical counselors included the prophetess Huldah (2 Kings 22:14), and her words recorded in verses 15–20 are both convicting and encouraging.

What did King Josiah request in his position of power—knees bowing to him? Far from it. He did not make much of his own authority but desired his people to acknowledge the authority equally over every person: the Lord and His Word. He essentially said, "the Lord will direct us; let us look to Him." King Josiah demonstrates that using power in a God-honoring manner requires kneeling before the One who has all authority and power, humbling oneself before other godly individuals, and directing allegiance to God.

By contrast, the interlopers of Jude's letter do not submit themselves to the authority of God, and they seek for others to ultimately be swayed by them—which is the cause of their divisiveness (Jude 19). While the Bible does not tell us if the interlopers responded repentantly, in the same spirit of King Josiah, to Jude's warnings, we do know that they start as those denying Christ's lordship and position as Master (Jude 4).

As Josiah's example shows us, our acceptance of God's ownership of our lives is reflected in our response to His law. This week, we will study Jude's writing on the false teachers' antinomianism, or lawlessness, which will be further explained in day 1. Lawlessness has been designated the sin of the soul, and the soul is the part of man that is aware of self. We determine who or what will rule our lives in our soul. For that reason, the denial of Christ's "lordship is the fundamental sin of the soul—the seat of our thoughts, our emotions, our will, our self-consciousness."[1]

Delineating Antinomianism

IDENTIFIER	TYPE OF SIN	PART OF MAN
Lawlessness (Greek *anomia*)	Sin of the soul	The "self-conscious" part

Rejecting right authority (Jude 8), the false teachers are self-directing and, thus, become the focus of their own boasting (v. 16), ultimately creating division (v. 19) between the authority of God and the self-asserted authority of man.

But only when all people bow to God's authority one day (Phil. 2:10) will the world be as it should. "The God of the Bible looks on his world as a jealous God who will not share his glory with another. Jealous, not as though he needs us. Jealous because only when God is God to all his creatures can the world be put on its true axis."[2] And to God's authority we turn in day 1.

WEEK 3 | DAY 1

For certain people have crept in unnoticed who long ago were designated for this condemnation, ungodly people, who pervert the grace of our God into sensuality and deny our only Master and Lord, Jesus Christ.
JUDE 4

Cross reference: *Then Jesus came to them and said, "All authority in heaven and on earth has been given to me."*
MATTHEW 28:18 (NIV)

Father, to deny the worthiness of Jesus Christ to be Master and Lord with all authority is to deny who He is. Help me welcome Your rule and reign over my life.

UNDERSTANDING ANTINOMIANISM

You may not be familiar with the theological concept Jude writes of, "antinomianism." So let's examine it.

This concept understands the grace of the gospel as a reason to be freed from the moral law of Christ. Instead of understanding the moral law as a "ministry of death" (2 Cor. 3:7), if it is seen as a means of salvation *but* essential to knowing and following God as a believer (1 Cor. 9:21; Gal. 6:2), this unbiblical view understands grace to mean that no law should have a role in the Christian life. In the inner spirit, then, this view uses grace as a reason to refuse being mastered by our King.

The false teachers Jude describes are lawless, following a prescription for destruction and seeking no correction (v. 4). As believers who are eager to avoid the example of the false teachers and please our Father, then, we must want to welcome the law. Yet, how can we who are under grace be welcoming of law (Rom. 6:14)?

The moral law is distinct from other promises that speak to a specific time and place in that it is reassumed in the New Testament. With the exception of keeping the Sabbath (Col. 2:16), the New Testament repeats the moral law's commandments—often expanding our understanding of the commandments concerning what happens in the heart (see Matt. 5:17–35; 22:37–40). In the New Testament these commandments are in focus as they relate to the heart, as the Spirit comes to indwell the New Testament believer. Theologian Sinclair Ferguson helpfully juxtaposes the times of Sinai and the indwelling of the Spirit:

> As Moses ascended Mount Sinai and brought down the Law on tablets of stone, now Christ has ascended into the heavenly Mount, but in contrast to Moses, he has sent down the Spirit who rewrites the law not now merely on tablets of stone but in our hearts.[3]

The Spirit within leads us to a new understanding of God's moral commands—one that is not burdensome, but expressive of love toward Christ. Love compels us to follow the commands of God (John 14:15). For love, a fruit of the Spirit within us, tells us that if Christ hates sin, we want not to ask how close to sin we can be but how far we can instead strive toward what He loves.

My wise parents taught me from an early age that if I ever have a question about whether or not a choice would be morally acceptable to God, then why would I choose it? Why would I want to do anything I could not be confident would honor Christ? Inching around questionable choices would not allow me to walk forward in full faith—without which God cannot be pleased (Heb. 11:6). Also, it would consume my heart and mind, preventing me from running in the Christian life. Only in the way of God's commands can we run freely (Ps. 119:32; cf. Heb. 12:1).

We are unable to bring about our own salvation through obedience to the moral law—salvation is apart from the law (Rom. 3:28). But Scripture does not allow our theology of law to abruptly halt with that truth, for that would be to dismiss the law altogether—to be antinomian, or lawless—swiping away the necessity of Christ's obedience to the law, the worthiness of God to be obeyed in all of His holy will, and the love we are blessed to be able to show Him of obedience in response to His sacrifice.

Jude makes prevalent reference to the errors and evils of antinomianism—the chart below from Hesselgrave and Hesselgrave lists the verses.[4]

Theme of Antinomianism in Jude's Epistle

DESIGNATION:	ANOMIA—LAWLESSNESS, DENYING OUR LORD (V. 4)
Explanations and descriptions:	1. They "reject authority" (v. 8) 2. They boast about themselves (v. 16) 3. They "cause division" (v. 19)
Metaphors and analogies:	1. "Wild waves of the sea" (v. 13) 2. "Wandering stars" (v. 13)
Precursors and examples:	1. The Israelites of the Exodus (v. 5) 2. The angels who did not keep their first rule (v. 6) 3. The rebellion of Korah (v. 11)

In today's study questions, we will learn from the explanations and descriptions for Jude's references to lawlessness, as well as his metaphors and analogies. In days 2 through 4, we will make a study of the precursors and examples Jude employs to help us understand lawlessness. And finally, in day 5, we will examine law in the context of mercy.

FOR STUDY *and* REFLECTION

Why is obedience to God's commandments intrinsic to being a follower of Christ? See Matthew 22:37–40 and 28:20 and the chart below.

New Testament Commands Based on Old Testament Ten Commandments

NEW TESTAMENT	OLD TESTAMENT (EXODUS 20)
Then Jesus said to him, "Be gone, Satan! For it is written, "'You shall worship the Lord your God and him only shall you serve'" (Matt. 4:10).	1. You shall have no other gods before me.
"But I say to you, Do not take an oath at all, either by heaven, for it is the throne of God, or by the earth, for it is his footstool, or by Jerusalem, for it is the city of the great King" (Matt. 5:34–35). "Are they not the ones who blaspheme the honorable name by which you were called?" (James 2:7).	3. You shall not take the name of the LORD your God in vain.

"Or do you not know that the unrighteous will not inherit the kingdom of God? Do not be deceived: neither the sexually immoral, nor idolaters, nor adulterers, nor men who practice homosexuality, nor thieves, nor the greedy, nor drunkards, nor revilers, nor swindlers will inherit the kingdom of God" (1 Cor. 6:9–10).

"They were filled with all manner of unrighteousness, evil, covetousness, malice. They are full of envy, murder, strife, deceit, maliciousness. They are gossips, slanderers, haters of God, insolent, haughty, boastful, inventors of evil, disobedient to parents, foolish, faithless, heartless, ruthless" (Rom. 1:29–31).

2. You shall not make for yourself a carved image [i.e., idolatry] . . . you shall not bow down to them or serve them.
5. Honor your father and your mother.
6. You shall not murder.
7. You shall not commit adultery.
8. You shall not steal.
10. You shall not covet.

"Therefore, having put away falsehood, let each one of you speak the truth with his neighbor, for we are members one of another" (Eph. 4:25).

9. You shall not bear false witness against your neighbor.

How does Christ transform your perspective of the moral law? See Romans 8:3–6.

Read 1 John 3:4 and 2 Thessalonians 3:4. To avoid antinomianism, believers submit to the authority of Christ as our personal authority. In your self-aware part, your soul, do you consider yourself under the authority of Christ?

Is that a choice you have made? Describe the circumstances of your making this decision.

Complete the chart below to understand Jude's metaphors and analogies concerning lawlessness.

Jude's Metaphors and Analogies for Lawlessness

JUDE'S DESCRIPTION OF INTERLOPERS	CROSS REFERENCE	HOW CAN I BE DIFFERENT THAN THE INTERLOPERS?
"wild waves of the sea, casting up the foam of their own shame" (v. 13a)	"But the wicked are like the tossing sea; for it cannot be quiet, and its waters toss up mire and dirt" (Isa. 57:20).	
"wandering stars, for whom the gloom of utter darkness has been reserved forever" (v. 13b)	"A man who wanders from the way of understanding will rest in the assembly of the dead" (Prov. 21:16 NASB).	

WEEK 3 | DAY 2

Now I want to remind you, although you once fully knew it, that Jesus, who saved a people out of the land of Egypt, afterward destroyed those who did not believe.

JUDE 5

Cross references: *Read Exodus 32 and Numbers 14:26–38; 26:64–65.*

Father, I want to avoid self-focus, grumbling, and hunger for power; I want to exalt You with faith and honor for Your ultimate power. Mold my heart according to the new birth You have worked within me by the Holy Spirit.

DISMISSING GOD'S AUTHORITY

Referring to Old Testament times when the Israelites worshiped a man-made golden calf instead of God and became faithless desert grumblers (see Ex. 32; Num. 14:26–38; 26:64–65), Jude writes that God[5] destroyed those who did not believe—teaching us that the one who saves is also the one who judges.

Scripture indicates that God's children "are not of those who shrink back and are destroyed, but of those who have faith and preserve their souls" (Heb. 10:39). We might surmise, then, that Israel was always shrinking back from God, ever at the edge of God's impending destruction. But consider their seeming spiritual health after crossing the Red Sea:

> Thus the Lord saved Israel that day from the hand of the Egyptians, and Israel saw the Egyptians dead on the seashore. Israel saw the great power that the Lord used against the Egyptians, so the people feared the Lord, and they believed in the Lord and in his servant Moses. —Exodus 14:30–31

Jude compares the false teachers and these Israelites: the people who witnessed miraculous signs are the very people who met God's destruction. They saw power of the Lord, feared God, and had this expression of belief—and yet, with all of that spiritual experience, their kind of faith receded to grumbling and disobedience (see Ps. 106:25).

To any reader feeling terrified about the destruction of these Israelites—as Martin Luther suggests, indeed, "This example he [Jude] gives to warn and terrify."[6] Fear is appropriate, as Hebrews confirms: "it is a fearful thing to fall into the hands of the living God" (Heb. 10:31).

I submit: Who could possibly be helped by the warnings of Scripture being veiled? Personally, I cannot in good conscience cushion this fear, for with all compassion I want you to see it that I might snatch you from it, if needed (Jude 23).

Fear is appropriate if your faith is the kind that has seen God's power, and yet grumbles and ignores His holy ways.

It is appropriate if your faith is the kind that has heard of the salvation of God and expressed trust through praying a prayer, without caring for obedience to Him.

It is appropriate if your faith is the kind that had allowed you to believe God would help you in a past difficult time, while now you dismiss Jesus as your Lord and Master.

None of us truly knows the heart of another—only God does—but I pray for each of you reading this what I pray for myself: to carefully examine ourselves.

After sober examination, the born-again person who is carnal (1 Cor. 3:1–3) will prayerfully be awakened to loving responses of obedience to the Lord before whom he or she will one day stand for evaluation (not condemnation)—able to anticipate greater heavenly rewards through new good works (1 Cor. 3:15; cf. Matt. 16:27).

The one who is not born again from above by the Spirit will, prayerfully, be saved from leaving the church and her people, revealed as one who never belonged (1 John 2:19; Acts 20:30). Such a one can be saved from destruction by turning to God—for anyone who believes in the *Lord* will be saved (1 John 4:15).

Now, our works (or lack thereof) might rightly prompt self-examination. But after this prompting, we can follow the wisdom of Paul: "Examine yourselves, to see whether you are in the faith. Test yourselves. Or do you not realize this about yourselves, that Jesus Christ is in you?—unless indeed you fail to meet the test!" (2 Cor. 13:5).

He commends first asking ourselves what we believe about Jesus Christ, essentially determining whether our beliefs are in accordance with "the faith." Second, he asks us to test whether we have been born again by the Spirit to new life, indwelt with Him. Both instructions turn our attention to Jesus Christ, King of kings and Lord of lords, Savior and Judge. Humbly meditating on Him and His free gift of salvation prompts faith-filled (not faithless) obedience in gratitude (not grumbling) by the Spirit.

I pray we may be the true spiritual children of Israel, a nation through which all others of the earth are blessed in Christ, able to "sing the Red Sea song of triumph,"[7] foreshadowing our New Covenant salvation, in true faith!

FOR STUDY *and* REFLECTION

Read 1 Corinthians 10:9–10. How is grumbling and complaining against God dismissive of God's authority over your life?

Read Psalms 95:10–11 and 106:24–25.

Describe a heart opposite to those of Israelites described in these verses, a heart not characterized by antinomianism—not disregarding the ways of God.

Read Jude 5 again, and also read verses 17–19. Evidently, the apostles' teaching of the faith included warnings that people would fall from the truth and consequences would come for those with empty "faith." Were you taught this when you became a believer? Reflect on why Scripture presents this teaching as important.

Read 2 Corinthians 13:5. How do you react?

Reflect: *Have I ever imagined that my faith would be stronger if I could be a witness to Old Testament miracles?*

In what way did this not turn out to be true of the Old Testament Israelites? Why do you think that is?

Read Ezekiel 36:26. What miracle discussed in this verse is greater than the parting of the Red Sea?

WEEK 3 | DAY 3

And the angels who did not stay within their own positions of authority, but left their proper dwelling, he has kept in eternal chains under gloomy darkness until the judgment of the great day . . .
JUDE 6

Cross references: Read Genesis 6:1–4 and Isaiah 14:12–15.

Father, the Day of Judgment is coming swiftly. Help me view You accordingly—high and mighty, unchangeable in authority, excellent and praiseworthy.

ABANDONING GOD'S AUTHORITY

In this intriguing verse, 6, Jude writes of angels who did not stay within their positions of authority. Perhaps this is a reference to angels who fell into sin generally (potentially with Isa. 14:12–15 as background).

Interpretations of Genesis 6:1–4—which is not an easily explained passage—have been suggested that identify "sons of God" as angels, beings that took any women they chose as wives. Other interpretations do not, and Jude may or may not be referring to this passage of Genesis in Jude 6. But if he is, we can note that he uses the Greek *angeloi*, which in nearly every case in the New Testament pertains to angels.[8] Therefore, interpretations of Genesis 6:1–4 that do not pertain to angels are irrelevant to our study, except in the case of two scenarios. First, some fuse two understandings of these first four verses of Genesis 6; that instead of appearing as humans, fallen angels possessed human nobility when taking whichever wives they chose. Second, if a nonangelic interpretation of this passage was to be certain, we could preclude this passage as being potential background for Jude—however, this does not appear conclusive.[9]

For the purposes of our studies, we can simply note that not enough information is provided to specify Jude's background with absolute certainty. Yet, to understand Jude's main point, we do not need to know more than what he has written. The judgment of these fallen angels is certain.

Scholar Thomas Schreiner writes, "The angels abandoned 'their own home' (*to idion oikētērion*) and transgressed proper bounds."[10] They have left their own places of God-given belonging and appointment, and they have diverged into forbidden areas not designated by God for them. When they do not keep themselves in God's ways, God keeps them for judgment:

> There is a bit of irony here, for "keep" *(tērēsantos)* is the same verb as that used for God's keeping them in darkness *(tetērēken)*, in each case meaning to "protect," "keep," or "guard."[11]

Jude writes of the coming day of the Lord's judgment, and *The Holman Illustrated Bible Dictionary* defines the "Day of the Lord" as "a point in time in which God displays His sovereign initiative to reveal His control of history, of time, of His people, and of all people."[12] The play on the word "keep" in Jude 6 reminds us that, in God's sights, abandoning the realm of His authority is ultimately impossible (cf. Jude 4).

For Study *and* Reflection

Based on Isaiah 14:12–15 and/or Genesis 6:1–4, describe a heart opposite to what is portrayed in these verses—a heart not characterized by antinomianism; a heart that is not abandoning the authority of God.

What in these examples helps us avoid sin?

Jude writes that the angels did not keep themselves in the realm of authority God gave (Jude 6). Keeping oneself beneath the authority of God—contrary to the example of the fallen angels—is evidence of a life that is kept for Jesus Christ (v. 2). How is keeping under Christ's authority connected to persevering in the faith?

When has your faith grown because you chose to submit to God instead of to the world?

According to Jude 6, angels are kept "until the judgment of the great day." Read Joel 2:11, 31; Zephaniah 1:14–16; and Malachi 4:1–3. Dwell on the future coming of the Day of the Lord and list truths of God's character that can be observed.

Woe to them! For they . . . perished in Korah's rebellion.
JUDE 11

Cross references: Read Numbers 16:1–3, 31–35 and Psalm 106:16–17.

Father, how I hate every string of conceit within me. Conceit births jealousy, which births rebellion, which leads to destruction. Help me hate these like You hate them. Help me, instead, to love humility, honoring others and Your authority, which leads to life.

USURPING GOD'S AUTHORITY

The account of Korah is told in Numbers 16:1–40, during the time of the Israelites' wandering in the wilderness following their exodus from Egypt. This man sought to usurp the authority God had given to Aaron and Moses to lead the Israelites (see Num. 16:1–3, 31–35). Though Moses had been given his authority by God (Ex. 4:10–17), Korah rebelled against Moses as God's spokesman. He stirred others, "250 chiefs of the congregation" (Num. 16:2), to stand with him in revolt.

Numbers 26:9–10 clarifies that Korah's rebellion was considered by God to be in direct conflict with not only Moses and Aaron but also with Himself: they "contended against Moses and Aaron . . . when they contended against the LORD." Jude advocates contending for the Lord's truth; Korah and his company contended against it.

In week 2, we explored the spirit from which contending comes for the Christian and learned that direct words can come from a gentle spirit. Now we learn that the spirit from which direct words proceed is not the single qualification of being a right contender in God's eyes. Contending must also be for truth. In the case of Jude, contending was on the basis of apostolic authority (Jude 3, 17).

The interlopers of Jude's day were like Korah: they opposed God's authority, slicing the truth and inserting assertions based on their own assumptions and posited authority. Lest we assume Jude believes this to be a minor infraction, he refers us to Korah's destruction. Those who unrepentantly set themselves toward usurping the authority of God, subtly wanting to have sway over creating the truth, will be swallowed:

> The ground under them split apart. And the earth opened its mouth and swallowed them up, with their households and all the people who belonged to Korah and all their goods. So they and all that belonged to them went down alive into Sheol, and the earth closed over them, and they perished from the midst of the assembly.—Numbers 16:31–33

Because of this rebellion, in Jewish thought, Korah "became the classic example of the antinomian heretic."[13] Charles Spurgeon also recommends we understand this story in the same way: "Look you, bold boasters of your own merits . . . this is the full-blown development of your rebellious self-conceit."[14] The dramatic image of the rebellious being consumed is especially helpful when considering the outward appearance of Korah prior to his destruction—he made himself appear as one who was serving in the interest of God's people:

> [Korah and his men] assembled themselves together against Moses and against Aaron and said to them, "You have gone too far! For all in the congregation are holy, every one of them, and the LORD is among them. Why then do you exalt yourselves above the assembly of the LORD?"—Numbers 16:3

What emotional pull is in these words! *Moses, you are not helping us. God is here among all of us—you and me, and those in our hearing! Why do we need you as our appointed leader?* "Yeah, why?" we might ask. Because God, the Ruler of all, had appointed the authority Korah sought to usurp—Korah dismissed God's word instead of pointing people to it. This example begs us to consider: *Would I have been led astray by the emotional plea that seemed considerate and in favor of me and the congregation—yet, against God's authority?* With the ground-opening wrath of God set against Korah's group, it is a sobering question.

FOR STUDY *and* REFLECTION

The historian Josephus described Korah's speech as a "malignant design, but with plausible words."[15] Read 2 Timothy 2:15–19. Why should believers oppose false teaching, especially when false teachers' words can seem favorable and helpful?

According to 2 Timothy 2:15–19, what are characteristics of false teaching?

What instruction did Paul give Timothy for avoiding false teaching (2 Tim. 2:15)?

How would you evaluate yourself as one capable of spotting rebellion hidden behind appealing words?

We can find a parallel between Korah desiring to worship God under his own authority aside from Moses and Aaron, whom God appointed, and those who claim to worship God today without submitting to Christ, whom God sent. From what you know and understand of Scripture, why cannot a person who has rejected Christ be a genuine worshiper of God?

Jude writes of the interlopers: "Woe to them!" (v. 11). See Matthew 23:13–39, and note Jesus' list of "woes." How do Jesus' words connect to Jude's heart in warning the church about the interlopers?

WEEK 3 | DAY 5

May mercy, peace, and love be multiplied to you.
JUDE 2

"Depth of Mercy! can there be" *by Charles Wesley*

Depth of mercy! Can there be
mercy still reserved for me?
Can my God His wrath forbear?
Me, the chief of sinners, spare?

I have long withstood His grace:
long provoked Him to His face;
would not hearken to His calls;
grieved Him by a thousand falls.

I my Master have denied,
I afresh have crucified,
oft profaned His hallowed name,
put Him to an open shame.

There for me the Savior stands,
shows His wounds and spreads His hands:
God is love! I know, I feel;
Jesus weeps, but loves me still!

Now incline me to repent!
Let me now my fall lament!
Now my foul revolt deplore!
Weep, believe, and sin no more.[16]

MERCY MULTIPLIED

For two semesters as a college student in Chicago, I was a weekly volunteer at
a Christian afterschool program in Cabrini-Green, a public housing project. I

witnessed children come to Christ, resulting in lives changed for eternity. I saw one little boy in particular share the gospel with some of his peers with such genuine urgency that he provided me with a lasting impression of how evangelism is done well—with sincerity, unwavering earnestness, and dedication to truth.

One day at the program, I had an opportunity to speak with the girls I had come to know during our weeks together. "You see, Jesus means so much to me. I want you to be able to know how good He is."

I had their attention.

Continuing, I shared some assorted aspects of my testimony and concluded with something like, "Jesus loves the world so much that He gave His Son to save us, to die on the cross for us. To accept this gift of salvation, you can pray, 'Jesus, I believe that I need You, and that You died on the cross to save me from my sin that separates me from You, and I want You to take control of my life.'"

One of the girls asked, "That's it?"

Her nonchalant response communicated the ease with which she believed she could simply repeat words for "salvation," not relief that her burden of sin could wonderfully be removed on the basis of Jesus Christ's sacrificial death and resurrection.

I wanted to share with these girls how much Jesus meant to me—that He is the best I have in this life and the one to come. But in the end, they received from me a context-less Christ and incomplete prayer. The concept of hell, wrath, and punishment due to the holiness of our Creator, who has every right to us in every way, had never entered our conversation; I had not given these girls the opportunity to appreciate what Christ had done and the full significance of Him coming to earth in love for us while we were still sinners. I shared my testimony and planted some seeds that day, but I failed to share the full gospel message. How might have their understanding of mercy been multiplied—enabling a fitting "That's it?" of awe—if I had said more? Does this example not also reflect us who believe too—that the more we comprehend the wrath of God, the more we thoroughly appreciate the mercy of God and live in its light?

Obscure God's supreme authority and holy standards, and the gospel becomes distorted. When hearers are ignorant to impending judgment, mercy has no context. In addition to Jude's wish-prayer for the mercy of God to be multiplied to his readers (Jude 2), Jude again directs his readers' attention to the mercy of God toward the conclusion of his epistle as they are waiting "for the mercy of our Lord Jesus Christ that leads to eternal life" (v. 21).

Waiting for mercy might sound strange to the ears of those who know they have been born again to new life in Christ. Yet, it will be at the final judgment that mercy will be fully known. In the future, all believers will experience the mercy of God when, upon seeing Christ our Creator and Judge, we gain a supreme awareness of our pardon. I can no longer remember what brother or sister in Christ mused with me that, perhaps, some tears that Christ will need to wipe away in glory (Isa. 25:8; cf. Rev. 21:4) will come from newly comprehending personal unfaithfulness in contrast with His steadfast grace.

A hopeful expectation of the mercy of God, our present joy in the gospel, and our ability to effectively share the gospel are possible through a right view of the law. The law is utterly useless to save—"Now the law came in to increase the trespass" (Rom. 5:20a)—but useful to make us aware of our need for Christ: "through the law comes knowledge of sin" (Rom. 3:20).

And the law continues to be useful to help us know the ways of God: "So the law is holy, and the commandment is holy and righteous and good" (Rom. 7:12). Without an awareness of the law, how could we rejoice in the mercy of being sent a Christ to fulfill the law (Matt. 5:17–20)?

How could we appreciate what Paul writes about upholding the law (Rom. 3:31)?

How could we rejoice in the mercy of now having the law written on our hearts by the Holy Spirit to powerfully save us from more unrighteousness in our daily lives in love of God our King (Jer. 31:33)?

Or how could we rejoice that before the holy standards of God we will one day be sustained in the presence of God through the mercy of Christ's blood covering us perfectly and completely (Jude 21)? Knowing the authority of the Lord and His holy standards, may mercy be multiplied to our hearts and minds—and overflow toward those with whom we share the good news.

For Study *and* Reflection

Reflect: When you share the gospel, is it with or without conveying the authority of Christ?

Can you think of some examples?

Reviewing verses and truths from this week, an awareness of the mercy of the Lord can be multiplied to the heart and mind. Read the verses below and compose a prayer of response according to these prompts and verses, as applicable to you.

God's Mercy in Light of Personal Lawlessness

REFERENCES	MERCY MULTIPLIED TO ME	PRAYER OF RESPONSE TO GOD'S MERCY
Matthew 28:18; Philippians 2:9–10	To You belongs all authority, even when I have not followed You.	
Numbers 14:34–35	I have been dismissive of Your authority.	
Jude 6	I have sought to abandon Your authority.	
Psalm 106:16–17	I have sought to usurp Your authority.	
2 Kings 22:11	Mercifully, Your Word convicts me and helps me welcome Your authority within my soul.	
Titus 3:5; Romans 5:20	Mercifully, Jesus has fulfilled the law in my place when the law made sin increase for me.	
Jude 21	Mercifully, I will stand before You in Christ and be spared all judgment.	
Revelation 21:4	Mercifully, You will wipe the tears from my eyes and replace them with eternal joy in Christ's works.	
Psalm 119:77, 156	Mercifully, Your Word tells me Your marvelous moral law builds fruitful righteousness in me and brings goodness and purity to my understanding.	
Ezekiel 11:19–20; John 14:15	Mercifully, Your Spirit enables me to follow Your ways with great love and honor for who You are, Master and Lord.	

Read John 15:10 and 2 John 6. What goodness does Christ desire and deserve in response to our being reborn?

Read Psalm 119:32. If you are born again, how are you free, according to this verse?

Read Philippians 2:9–10, Ephesians 1:21, Acts 2:33, and Matthew 28:18. Make a list of reasons for Christ's worthiness as King.

Keeping the Spirit

My favorite references for the topic of reverence toward the Lord are not theological treatises, commentaries, or sermons. Rather, in filling my days with truth, my best sources largely wrote my growing years: my godly parents.

They taught me to not flippantly shout "Hallelujah," because this word means "praise to the Lord," and it is to be said with full sincerity. They taught me to not create nonsensical words to songs about Jesus, for our words about Him were to be based on the truth of Scripture—and also to not sing about the Lord in a thoughtless, silly way that made little of what I was saying. We prayed before meals—not due to mere formality, habit, or sentimentality but because we wanted to honor our Lord who gave us that day, that day's food, and much more. We prayed before trips, asking God for His traveling mercies because we knew He held our lives. We watched only a little television because so much was (and is) filled with what God hates and therefore could not be enjoyed.

As a child, I understood that my parents would probably be considered strict by many of my friends who, I presumed, often had very different home contexts than I did—but even then, I was only glad. This was not senseless rigidity. The instruction I received was the result of an undeniable reverence and worship in my parents. Word by word, prayer by prayer—one heartfelt conversation and correction at a time focused on Jesus Christ and what He lovingly deserves because of who He is and what He has done for us—my mother and father taught me the principle of God being the supreme, holy Person before whom we live each decision, each

day. Their instruction was not about controlling my behavior, or even primarily about me at all; it was about turning toward God and honoring Him in our home and lives.

In *God in the Whirlwind*, David Wells writes, "Where we want to be is before God," and he quotes Psalm 16:8, "I have set the LORD always before me."[1] This is godliness, the heart of reverence. For *ir*reverence little looks to God, barely lives before Him, and therefore rarely executes daily life based on God's true worth. One definition of irreverence follows.

> A complete absence of the proper sense of awe, respect and wonder that is inspired and demanded by the character and activity of the living God. Irreverence involves disrespect for the character, deeds, words, law, and ministers of God. As such, it brings judgment upon those who behave in this way.[2]

In week 3 of our study, we examined that in our souls—the "self-conscious" part of us—we determine who or what will have mastery over us. We learned that because God is our authority, and all the world is God's, no one can ultimately escape Him—whether we bow before Him now willingly, or when He appears, since all will then acknowledge His kingship. Now, just as our souls cannot escape the realm of God's authority, we also cannot ultimately escape the demands of His objective, supreme worth. This is the basis for reverence. This central theme of reverence, or godliness, in Jude concerns our spirits, the "God-conscious" part of us.[3] Jude teaches us about avoiding *un*godliness and *ir*reverence and replacing them with their opposites.

Delineating Irreverence

IDENTIFIER	TYPE OF SIN	PART OF MAN
Ungodliness, impiety, irreverence (Greek *aesbeia*)	Sin of the spirit	The "God-conscious" part

The interlopers of Jude's context did not revere God in their spirits (Jude 4), and Jude writes more about the ensuing judgment for their behaviors in the passages we examine this week. They had not submitted to the greatness of God and arranged their spirits according to this reality.

As I mentioned, the examples of my parents' displays of reverence came from a foundation of scriptural thought about how to regard God based on who He is. You and I often hear the word "God"—to our regret, we frequently hear His name profaned. But even a fresh consideration of God being *God* can help us reflect on what He is due. To that end, we begin our week of study.

WEEK 4 | DAY 1

*For certain people have crept in unnoticed who
long ago were designated for this condemnation,
ungodly people, who pervert the grace of our God
into sensuality and deny our only Master and Lord,
Jesus Christ.*

JUDE 4

Cross reference: *Oh come, let us worship and bow down; let us kneel
before the LORD, our Maker! For he is our God, and we are the people of his
pasture, and the sheep of his hand.*

PSALM 95:6–7

*Father, a lack of respect and honor for who You are and what You have done is pervasive
in and around me. Let me honor You all of my days; You are my God. I set You before me.*

UNDERSTANDING IRREVERENCE

Irenaeus wrote: "those are ungodly who worship not the God that truly is."[4] A
sense of awe and respect in our spirits is lost when we deny the God who is there.
Setting our spirits fittingly before Him to worship with our lives, David Wells
recommends:

We must come back to our first principles. And the most basic of these is the fact that God is there and that he is objective to us. He is not there to conform to us; we must conform to him. He summons us from outside of ourselves to know him. We do not go inside of ourselves to find him. We are summoned to know him only on his terms. He is not known on our terms. This summons is heard in and through his Word. It is not heard through our intuitions.[5]

Wells mentions a number of points here. In summary, first, God exists, and He is objective to us, meaning He is who He is, unchanged by our intuitions and senses about Him. Wells clarifies that though God is not found in our intuitions, faith in God is a personal response to Him that arises from our inner selves.[6] Second, God is outside of us and found on His terms, through His Word. In this study, we have been examining the importance of the faith, Scriptural doctrinal content; it teaches us that God is great and greatly to be praised for all He is and has done for us (Ps. 145:3a). His greatness is to shape how we worship Him.

As we study the Word, submit to it, and adopt God's being and character as above us, personal intuitions and feelings become less and less what steer our lives. God's Word begins to take its prime place in us, and we realize that worship acceptable to God is that which lines up with what we know of Him through Scripture. We start with Him, rather than with ourselves, beginning our worship with professing who He is before focusing on our needs and desires. We come to see that if we once thought it God's greatest duty to satisfy our needs and wants, we were mistaken. We are beholden, first and foremost, to Him and what He asks of us.

"Oh come, let us worship and bow down; let us kneel before the LORD, our Maker! For he is our God, and we are the people of his pasture, and the sheep of his hand." These inviting words from Psalm 95:6–7 capture the essence of reverent worship. We worship, bow, and kneel because He is Lord, Maker, and God. And we belong to His pasture, His hand. Knowing these impetuses for worship, the question starts to arise within us: *What can we bring—what can we offer this great God?* Of course, we add nothing to God who has given us all and is complete in Himself, and we add nothing to our salvation, which was solely purchased by the precious blood of Jesus.

Still, God accepts our heartfelt sacrifices—our very lives are to be lived in response to Christ's sacrifice (Rom. 12:1). Wells suggests that "Without the knowledge of God in those who worship, without active faith, without reverence, without gratitude in the worshiper, even the best forms of worship simply fall flat."[7] When freed from the consuming confines of our own earthly feelings, needs, and desires, we become worshipers with offerings, such as study, reverence, gratitude, and love for God and others, that guide our attitudes, desires, behaviors, and prayers. With God in focus, when we hear of a biblical Christianity that is "deep, costly, and demanding,"[8] we can say—by God's grace and for His sake—*Yes, let me follow that way. God is worthy; let me kneel, let me bow, and let me be a living sacrifice in praise.*

Jude calls the interlopers of his day "ungodly people" (v. 4)—people who refuse to worship the God who is, who do not accept His definitions, who are not willing to sacrifice their own wants for God's glorious light, who do not bow to the worthy God who owns them. In a display of fitting reverence for God, Jude speaks forth what they are doing that is so dismissive of the holy, majestic One—and using various examples and explanations, we will learn to understand what reverence is and is not.

Theme of Irreverence in Jude's Epistle[9]

DESIGNATION:	*AESBEIA*—UNGODLINESS, IMPIETY, IRREVERENCE (V. 4)
Explanations and descriptions:	1. "Revile angelic majesties" (v. 8 NASB) 2. "Revile [speak abusively]" (v. 10 NASB) 3. "Ungodly deeds which they have done" (v. 15 NASB) 4. "Grumblers, finding fault" (v. 16 NASB) 5. "Mockers" (v. 18 NASB)
Metaphor:	1. "Hidden reefs in your love feasts" (v. 12 NASB)
Precursors and examples:	1. The people of the Exodus (v. 5) 2. Michael the archangel (v. 9) 3. The way of Cain (v. 11)

In day 2, we will study Michael, the archangel. In day 3, we will examine the way of Cain. In day 4, we will learn from the prophecy of Enoch. And in day 5, we will learn about the duo of reverence and peace. Other verses on the chart about irreverence above we will survey in the questions for study and reflection today and in week 5.

For Study *and* Reflection

Read Jude 5 and 16. In week 3, day 2, we studied Jude 5 and the destruction of the Israelites. Read again the description of irreverence provided in this week's introduction, page 89. Why is grumbling and finding fault with God's ways contrary to a godly, reverent spirit?

Complete the chart below to study Jude's metaphor concerning irreverence.

Jude's Metaphors for Irreverence

JUDE'S DESCRIPTION OF INTERLOPERS	NOTES AND CROSS REFERENCES:	HOW CAN I BE OPPOSITE OF THE INTERLOPERS?
"These are hidden reefs at your love feasts." (v. 12a)	According to MacArthur, "Reefs are undersea coral formations usually located close to the shore. They are potentially harmful to ships because they can rip open the bottoms of their hulls, causing the vessels to sink."[10] Also, according to Schreiner, "During love feasts the early Christians shared a meal together that probably was consummated by the celebration of the Lord's Supper (1 Cor. 11:17–34; Acts 2:42, 46)."[11]	
"as they feast with you without fear." (v. 12b)	"Now the Spirit expressly says that in later times some will depart from the faith by devoting themselves to deceitful spirits and teachings of demons, though the insincerity of liars whose consciences are seared." (1 Tim. 4:1–2)	

Refer to Psalm 95:6–7. How do you approach God? Is your manner appropriate when you consider His greatness and supreme worth?

When our wants and sense of need are conformed to what He asks of us, the nature of our prayers, as we mature spiritually, becomes more fitting and reverent. Have you noticed this in your own life? What do you regularly pray about?

Read Romans 12:1. What does God ask of His followers?

Ask yourself: *How am I living in this way already, and how can I grow?*

*But when the archangel Michael, contending with
the devil, was disputing about the body of Moses,
he did not presume to pronounce a blasphemous
judgment, but said, "The Lord rebuke you."*
JUDE 9

Cross reference: *And the Lᴏʀᴅ said to Satan, "The Lᴏʀᴅ rebuke you, O Satan!
The Lᴏʀᴅ who has chosen Jerusalem rebuke you!"*
ZECHARIAH 3:2a

*Father, I want to know more about reverence; I want to have a sense for how I am to
regard You rightly. Teach me, Lord.*

A GENUINE SHOW OF REVERENCE

The dispute Jude references in verse 9 concerning the body of Moses is recorded in
a noncanonical, apocryphal book called *The Assumption of Moses*. Apocryphal writings are those that have not been accepted in the canon of Scripture. Such writings
found in the first century ranged from historical and orthodox to fanciful. Hesselgrave and Hesselgrave state: "Jude's use of the incident does not confer historical

validity on all that is to be found in that book, but it does constitute a testimony to the factualness of that particular incident."[12] The ending to *The Assumption of Moses* is lost, yet it can be reconstructed: "After the death of Moses Michael came to bury his body. The devil (Samma'el, one of a variety of Jewish names for the devil) came and argued that the body should be given to him, for Moses had been a murderer (i.e., he had murdered the Egyptian, Exodus 2:12–14) and thus did not deserve an honorable burial."[13] Jude describes a scene in which Michael refrains from judging an accuser, who ultimately accused God that forgiveness would not come to Moses after all. Michael leaves this judgment of Satan to God, saying, "The Lord rebuke you" (Jude 9).

MacArthur, at this point in his commentary on Jude, notes the similarity between this account and an account in Scripture in Zechariah 3:2 in which the Angel of the Lord, considered to be the preincarnate Christ, deferred to the judgment of God the Father.[14] In Zechariah's vision, Satan is again seen as the accuser—this time of Joshua, a high priest in Old Testament times, one who had returned from exile (see Hag. 1:1).

Though Joshua had this position, still, before the holy throne of God, Joshua's garments are filthy and defiled. But in place of these, Joshua is given "pure vestments," his iniquity is taken away (Zech. 3:4). While Satan could accurately accuse Joshua of sins, Joshua had been plucked into purity by Christ (Zech. 3:2). Therefore, Satan's accusation no longer has any footing, due to the justification of Joshua. Despite the clean garments, the Angel of the Lord yet leaves judgment of Satan to the Father in reverence for the apparent order that existed,[15] as does Michael in Jude's direct reference.

This display of genuine reverence is dramatic. We may be tempted to irreverently grumble against the structures God has instituted or His timing in fulfilling His plans for this world, especially as these infringe on our sense of comfort, happiness, or control. Yet, if Michael and the preincarnate Christ did not pronounce judgment against *even Satan*, "the slightest disregard of the Divine Person . . . becomes unthinkable."[16]

FOR STUDY *and* REFLECTION

Read Zechariah 3:1–5 and 1 John 2:1. Why is focusing on sin in the believer's life to the exclusion of remembering Christ's sacrifice irreverence? Reflect: Do you focus on your sin without looking to Christ as your advocate before the Father? Do you focus on other believers' sin without considering the forgiveness that Christ has accomplished for them?

Read Matthew 5:39–40, Matthew 27:12–14, and Romans 12:9. When encountering the evil accusations of Satan against the complete and satisfactory provision of God for the forgiveness of sins in Christ, Michael and the Angel of the Lord reverently refrained from pronouncing judgment. According to these verses, why can a righteous God ask us to not be personally responsible for bringing others to justice in all situations?

As you consider the position and character of God, describe why He alone is worthy of being the One to ultimately decide how and when judgments are made.

Considering Zechariah 3:1–5 and the story of Moses's burial according to Jude 9, describe how Satan uses partial truth in a misleading way to accuse.

Does this motivate you to be discerning with all the messages you hear and receive? Explain.

When you meditate on Michael's and the Angel of the Lord's restraint from judgment, how are you compelled to revere God?

Woe to them! For they walked in the way of Cain . . .
JUDE 11a

Cross reference: *Read Genesis 4:1–16 and Hebrews 11:4.*

Father, You deserve all of me, including my heart. I thank You for the excellent sacrifice that Abel offered You of first fruits, exemplifying the godliness of considering himself and all he had to be Yours. By this sacrifice, he speaks truths to me today.

AN EMPTY SHOW OF REVERENCE

Jude mentions that the interlopers "walked in the way of Cain" (v. 11). What does he mean? Many have suggested that Cain disrespected God by creating his own type of sacrifice; a blood sacrifice was required by God instead of the vegetation sacrifice given by Cain.[17] However, in Leviticus 2–7 God indeed later requires both animal and vegetable sacrifices.

Others suggest that the envious murder of Abel by Cain indicates "an example of hatred of one's brothers and sisters."[18] D. A. Carson writes "In the immediate context of Jude, the false teachers do not love the truth 'once for all entrusted' to Christ's people, and this works itself out in animus to the Christians themselves (very much as in 1 John)."[19]

According to the apostle John, false teachers resemble Cain when he hated Abel and Abel's righteousness (1 John 3:12): "Everyone who hates his brother is a murderer, and you know that no murderer has eternal life abiding in him" (1 John 3:15). Perhaps Jude is suggesting that just as Cain murdered Abel, false teachers murder people's souls, as Douglas Moo puts it.[20]

In this, the false teachers use their disdain toward righteousness to lead others away from it as well. In Jude's context, the interlopers were still admitted to the church, seemingly indistinguishable from members of the true church (Jude 12). In 1 John 2, the false teachers had already gone out from among the congregation (v. 19), making their hatred of the church apparent. The interlopers in Jude's context take pleasure in leading others to their spurious viewpoints, taking souls who might have repented and believed in Christ, perhaps with an undercover envy of those who are truly born again.

Let us also consider another interpretation not based primarily on Cain's hatred, but earlier on his sacrifice itself. (By now focusing on another interpretation, I do not mean to preclude holding the previous 1 John interpretation as well, as the path of the interlopers of Jude's context. But it seems best to me to also consider the light of Hebrews 11:4 below. Jude's mention of Cain is brief, and he does not specify his exact thoughts and implications—and perhaps that is the point, to consider a full picture of this man.)

Hebrews 11:4 states, "By faith Abel offered to God a more acceptable sacrifice than Cain, through which he was commended as righteous, God commending him by accepting his gifts. And through his faith, though he died, he still speaks." Cain lacked faith:

> The reason for the different reception of the two offerings was the state of mind towards God with which they were brought, and which manifested itself in the selection of the gifts. Not, indeed, in the fact that Abel brought a bleeding sacrifice and Cain a bloodless one; for this difference arose from the difference in their callings, and each necessarily took his gift from the produce of his own

occupation. It was rather in the fact that Abel offered the fattest firstlings of his flock, the best that he could bring; whilst Cain only brought a portion of the fruit of the ground, but not the first-fruits. By this choice Abel . . . manifested that disposition which is designated faith [according to Hebrews 11:4].[21]

Cain evokes a way that seeks to keep up appearances of a strong relationship with God without the perceived nuisance of having a genuine, reverent, and righteousness-loving faith from the heart.[22] To him, good standing before God was a right he deserved following his works. But God summons the whole person—not merely for outer conformity to His ways, but for an inner spirit that sees obedience to God in good works as our privilege and joy just because they are for Him. In Jude's context, outward appearances were being maintained to a degree—the interlopers were still part of the congregation—but their hearts were faithless and far from God.

For Study *and* Reflection

Refer to Genesis 4:1–16 and Hebrews 11:4. Why is a faithless sacrifice irreverent? Reflect on how Cain's type of sacrifice disparages the sacrifice, kindness, love, omniscience, holiness, purity, and so on, of God.

One commentator writes that walking in Cain's way "includes the threat of sharing in Cain's judgment."[23] Jude continues to make reference to judgment. In accordance with week 3, day 2, as you carefully consider yourself, do you honor who Christ is, and have you experienced rebirth by the Spirit—or do you merely attempt to stay on good terms with God through superficial nods toward Him in your actions?

Or, as a born again believer, do you ever keep up appearances of a strong relationship with God without continuing to foster reverent faith in God from your heart?

Read Genesis 4:13–15. Even after being confronted directly by God, Cain is unrepentant. What is the subject of his focus, instead of his offense toward God?

Is your own repentance ever derailed by a similar attitude as Cain's?

Read Hebrews 11:4, but now consider Abel. In light of all you know about Cain, what hope does Abel's reverent way of life speak to you?

WEEK 4 | DAY 4

It was also about these that Enoch, the seventh from Adam, prophesied, saying, "Behold, the Lord comes with ten thousands of his holy ones, to execute judgment on all and to convict all the ungodly of all their deeds of ungodliness that they have committed in such an ungodly way, and of all the harsh things that ungodly sinners have spoken against him."

JUDE 14–15

Cross reference: *Enoch walked with God, and he was not, for God took him.*
GENESIS 5:24

Father, I confess that by my attitudes and actions, I often ignore Your greatness and worth. I elevate myself when I should humble myself. I disregard Your supremacy when I should submit to You with faith. Make me like Enoch who walked closely with You.

REVERENCE THAT CANNOT BE IGNORED

After Cain murdered his brother Abel, Adam and Eve were given another son who would follow in Abel's example of godliness: Seth (Gen. 4:25–26). A Redeemer had been promised to Adam and Eve after their earlier fall into sin, an offspring who would "bruise the head" of the serpent (Gen. 3:15)—directly following the fall, this is the first mention of biblical good news, which is called the protoevangelium. This Redeemer would not come from the line of Cain; He would come from the line of Seth (Luke 3:38), who exemplifies that because of God's goodness, hope exists even after the atrocities of human sin.

T. Desmond Alexander notes that "the contrast between the lines of Cain and Seth is striking."[24] After the account of Cain murdering Abel, the subject of offspring is in focus. Cain's line would include Lamech, a murderer (Gen. 4:23–24); and yet, from Seth's line would come Enoch, who walked with God and was taken to God's presence without death (Gen. 5:24). Cain was "of the evil one" (1 John 3:12). Alexander continues to observe: "Here we encounter the idea that human beings may by their actions be perceived as belonging either to the unrighteous 'offspring of the serpent' or to the righteous 'offspring of the woman'."[25] Our individual decisions about Christ can spiritually set us either in the line of Eve into which God introduced hope of a great Redeemer, or the line of the serpent in his deception and evil.

Jude introduces Enoch and his prophecy in verse 14 and, considering the symbolism surrounding the dichotomous lines of descent of Seth and Cain, it is no wonder that Jude clarifies he is speaking about Enoch, "the seventh from Adam," for in Genesis 4:17 we learn that Cain also had a son named Enoch. But from Enoch of the line of Seth we read a prophecy in Jude[26]—from this Enoch, whose godliness was extraordinary, we listen for spiritual wisdom.

To Jude's context, and to us, he speaks that the Lord will come. A promised Redeemer will crush the head of the serpent—but not only that, He will come in majesty to judge those who are "of the serpent" like Cain, whose ungodliness yields only faithless sacrifices devoid of devotion to their Creator God and whose envy of those who are godly leads to hatred, murderous intent, and to murder itself.

You and I, in times of suffering or when witness to evil, may also refer to the second coming of Christ: "Come, Lord Jesus" (Rev. 22:20). In nearness to the Lord, we express great hope in our Redeemer's victory, joy that His people will be delivered from evil, hope that no more evil will be permitted to exist without immediate justice, and joy for His name to be seen as holy and true by all. Yet, as Enoch indicates, we also implicitly ask for Christ to come with conviction and judgment for those who by their actions are still in the "line of the serpent." Enoch's prophecy comes to us even this day as a plea for spreading Christ's good news while opportunity remains; for anyone who would make full commitment to Christ as Lord and Savior can be reborn into the spiritual family of God, saved from the dying serpent's line.

FOR STUDY *and* REFLECTION

Refer to Jude 14–15. Note each time Jude mentions ungodliness, and describe all of the ways Jude uses this word.

Read Genesis 4:23–24, and refer to Genesis 5:24. How would you contrast what is written about Lamech versus Enoch?

Read Hebrews 11:5 and refer to Jude 14–15. Enoch was commended in Scripture as one who greatly pleased God. According to Jude 14–15, Enoch faithfully prophesied difficult truth. In what way(s) does speaking God's truth to others require faith?

Read Revelation 22:14–21. According to verses 15, 18, and 19, how are people who are not ready for the coming of the Lord Jesus characterized?

How are people who are ready for the Lord Jesus' coming characterized? See verses 14, 17, 21.

The line of the serpent and his kingdom of darkness will soon be met with the finality of judgment upon the second coming of the Light of the world. How does reverence for Christ, or setting His kingdom before you as your foremost reality, give you courage to spread the gospel?

WEEK 4 | DAY 5

May mercy, peace, and love be multiplied to you.
JUDE 2

"Come to the Ark"

Come to the ark, come to the ark;
    To Jesus come away:
The pestilence walks forth by night,
    The arrows fly by day.

Come to the ark: the waters rise,
    The seas their billows rear;
While darkness gathers o'er the skies,
    Behold a refuge near!

Come to the ark, all, all that weep
    Beneath the sense of sin:
Without, deep calleth unto deep,
    But all is peace within.

Come to the ark, ere yet the flood
    Your lingering steps oppose;
Come, for the door which open stood,
    Is now about to close.[27]

PEACE MULTIPLIED

The thundering was soon over us. Ahead, brake lights were barely visible. How rain manages to fall from the skies horizontally, I have no idea. This was no ordinary storm—the next day would tell of its damage throughout the city. Tyler managed to exit the highway and pull up to a restaurant. Before parking, he dropped our daughter and me off at the front door, but even those few seconds from the car to the entrance gave us a good soaking.

Wiping beads of rain from my hair and waiting for Tyler so we could recap our happiness that, for a start, our brakes worked, tires did not skid, and the car did not hydroplane, I observed diners eating peacefully. Tyler emerged, and the server was ready to seat us.

And soon, we too were scooching our chairs into our table, exchanging smiles, and feeling enveloped in one another's company. Being inside a structure we were confident could withstand the storm quickly changed our experience.

By this point in our studies of Jude, we have read of a certitude that judgment is coming for the ungodly, for those who deny Jesus Christ as Master and Lord. And, rather than denying who He is, we have discussed that reverence for the Lord means setting Him before us and living all our days in view of the great God who has done great things for us.

God once judged the earth by water—but He promised not to do so again after Noah (Gen. 9:11). Now, flames are ahead (Jude 23). Yet, with Noah's story in mind and that first judgment of the world, "Interestingly, the early church presented Noah's ark as a symbol of Christ. Some of the earliest drawings of Christ are representations of an ark affixed to a cross."[28] Setting ourselves before Him, we know that we are held by the only vessel that can weather what is to come.

Our view of Christ grows; Jude's doxology, which we will study in week 6, exemplifies this reverent heart, ascribing to God "glory (credit), majesty (beauty), dominion (jurisdiction), and authority (power)."[29] While the interlopers are loud-mouthed boasters (v. 16), we know who really is deserving of our praise and adoration. While the interlopers seek to gain advantage and standing, we know who really has jurisdiction, kingship, and power but humbled Himself (Phil. 2:6–8). Judgment for the world is certain, but our Lord has already submitted willingly, for our sakes, to wrath—and risen.

Jude's wish-prayer included a desire for peace to be multiplied to his recipients—a greater understanding of this aspect of the grace of God. To the world, Jude is a terrifying book. Yet, to the Christian, as it dwells within us, Jude increases our spirits' confidence in Christ. The great God, the God beyond us and objective to us—on His terms, the only terms that matter, we can be welcomed in Christ, our ark. And "all is peace within."[30]

FOR STUDY and REFLECTION

How is peace multiplied to you through understanding Philippians 2:6–8?

How is peace multiplied to you through understanding Philippians 2:9–11?

Read Romans 5:1–2. Describe the foundation of your spirit's peace.

Read Jude 16–18. Describe every way and reason the interlopers must have been without peace.

How would this all change if they were to bow to Christ?

What is your spirit's disposition before God?

Read John 10:28–30. In light of Jude's passages of judgment, what is your reaction?

According to Hebrews 13:20–21, what does the great God of our peace, our great shepherd, expect of us? You might want to close out your study time today by personalizing these verses as a prayer.

Keeping the Body

If you have wrestled with this question—*How can a God of love consign anyone to hell?*—you are not alone. Many through the ages have asked the same. Damnation is a grim and disconcerting topic. But even more so, it is critical to both understanding grace and the present reality of mankind; we must study it.

In his systematic theology, scholar Robert Duncan Culver (1916–2015) outlines the biblical doctrine of the eternal state of the unsaved with five propositions.

1. The state of the lost in their final punishment is death.

2. The measure of the final punishment is deeds done in life.

3. The nature of the final punishment is torment.

4. The duration of the final punishment is everlasting.

5. The place of the final punishment is hell, also called the lake of fire and Gehenna.[1]

He continues:

When I first assembled this outline, late on a cold northern Ohio night, alone in a small church basement room with concrete walls, my feet cold, my hands numb, alone in the great building, my dear wife and two small sons snug in bed two miles away, the stillness undisturbed save for the hiss of the gas heater

and the annoying clack of the ancient typewriter, I shrank from every word I wrote. Even now in greater comfort there is no greater pleasure in the task, for the very atmosphere of this lovely autumn Sabbath seems deadly with the weight of the sinner's doom. Yet we approach it with the interest and respect due to all of God's revelations. What His Word teaches clearly we accept in faith even if the heart staggers and the mind reels.[2]

One action Jude desired for his letter to produce in its recipients was for them to "save others by snatching them out of the fire" (Jude 23). And we know already that Jude frequents the topic of judgment in his letter. The future judgment (not condemnation) of *believers* will be studied in week 6. In this introduction, we come to the sobering topic of hell for the unsaved.

Culver writes that his "lovely autumn Sabbath seem[ed] deadly." With those striking words, he reveals a true assessment of the condition of the unsaved. He also writes that "the heart staggers and the mind reels" when it comes to the doctrine of damnation. Yet, he sets an example of being faithful to Scripture, prioritizing doctrine above feelings. Others might have difficulty accepting this doctrine and, as Jude reminds us, we can "have mercy on those who doubt" (v. 22). Mercifully, we can recognize, as does Culver, the stunning impact of this truth and address the honest question: *How can a loving God condemn people to hell?*

In response: How can He not? We need not attempt to set God's love against His wrath. S. Lewis Johnson describes the two in relation to each other:

The God of the Bible is a God whose holy being is revolted by that which is a contradiction of his holiness, and he expresses his wrath in punitive justice. He loves enough to hate evil; in fact, his wrath is just that, the antagonism of holy love to evil. It is not a vindictive rage, nor is it an emotional reaction to irritated self-concern.[3]

Wrath exists in connection with God's holy love; though we can study God's characteristics separately, they do not exist distinctly from each other. God's love would not be perfect love without hatred of evil. How could it be otherwise for this infinitely holy Being? With this consideration, biblical love and licentiousness are incompatible. For if antinomianism views grace as a reason to ignore our King's commandments, licentiousness sees grace as a reason to largely give allowance to sin. Licentiousness is a dangerous doctrine that might produce false assurance of salvation in the lives of its adherents who assume that they have truly understood the gospel when believing it to be a reason to accept or allow personal sin because "Jesus will forgive anyway." This disposition toward God's lavish grace might, therefore, numb consciences, stifle repentance, and produce a focus purely on personal happiness through worldly means. Licentious teaching cloaks God's true character.

Delineating Licentiousness[4]

IDENTIFIER	TYPE OF SIN	PART OF MAN
Licentiousness (Greek *aselgeia*)	Sin of the body	The "world-conscious" part

Jude writes of false teachers who do precisely this; they are people "who turn the grace of our God into licentiousness" (Jude 4 NASB). However justified, these false teachers misunderstand the nature of grace and, placing a high regard on dealings in this present world, ignore the wrath of God and His promise of judgment. They perhaps presume a loving God of grace little cares about sins of the body, which make them happy and do not seem to hurt other people. But by His very nature revealed in Scripture, God does and must. Culver writes, "What His Word teaches clearly we accept in faith."[5] May we so strive, engaging mercifully with those who are doubting and, prayerfully, snatching others from the coming fire.

WEEK 5 | DAY 1

For certain people have crept in unnoticed who long ago were designated for this condemnation, ungodly people, who pervert the grace of our God into sensuality and deny our Master and Lord, Jesus Christ.

JUDE 4

Cross reference: *Now faith is the assurance of things hoped for, the conviction of things not seen.*

HEBREWS 11:1

Father, please give me faith in temptation. Please let me always see Your greatness that surpasses this world. I want to only be dominated by You, my gracious Master.

UNDERSTANDING LICENTIOUSNESS

The biblical word for licentiousness, or sensuality, in Jude, *aselgeia* in Greek, "is related to the sins of *greed*, *self-indulgence*, and *sexual immorality*. Note that those are *body*-centered, *flesh*-oriented, and *self*-gratifying."[6] Jude gives us various illustrations and descriptions concerning this sin.

Theme of Licentiousness in Jude's Epistle[7]

DESIGNATION:	*ASELGEIA*—LICENSE FOR IMMORALITY, SENSUALITY (V. 4)
Explanations and descriptions:	1. "By dreaming, defile the flesh" (v. 8 NASB) 2. Destroyed by "things . . . they know by instinct" (v. 10 NASB) 3. "Following after their own lusts" (v. 16 NASB) 4. "Flattering . . . for . . . advantage" (v. 16 NASB) 5. "Worldly minded" (v. 19 NASB)
Metaphors and analogies:	1. "Caring for [only] themselves" (v. 12 NASB) 2. "Clouds without water, carried along by winds" (v. 12 NASB) 3. "Autumn trees without fruit . . . uprooted" (v. 12 NASB) 4. "Wild waves of the sea" (v. 13)
Precursors and examples:	1. Sodom and Gomorrah (v. 7) 2. Balaam's error (v. 11)

Dreams, instincts, wildness, and being theologically uprooted from doctrine to chase fulfillment of the cravings of the heart and body depict a person ever being pulled along by undenied lusts. In *The Great Divorce*, C. S. Lewis writes:

> The sensualist, I'll allow ye, begins by pursuing a real pleasure, though a small one. His sin is the less. But the time comes on when, though the pleasure becomes less and less and the craving fiercer and fiercer, and though he knows that joy can never come that way, yet he prefers to joy the mere fondling of unappeasable lust and would not have it taken from him. He'd fight to the death to keep it. He'd like well to be able to scratch; but even when he can scratch no more he'd rather itch than not.[8]

In week 4, day 1, we examined God's existence outside of our feelings, emotions, and intuitions. Believing God's existence in this manner shows our reverence for Him and the Scripture He ordained to reveal Himself to us. And this week, we can note another application. When lured and overcome by self-indulgence, greed, or our cravings, we may not predominantly, or scarcely at all, feel or sense God. Lusts can blind our perceptions and hearts.

Thinking of the pull of these desires that Jude warns us to confront, Hebrews 11:1 comes to mind: "Now faith is the assurance of things hoped for, the conviction of things not seen." When we cannot see past our sins, we might actually fear being rid of desires and cravings that seem to be a part of us and who we are; but the answer is faith. We return to the conviction that the worth and authority of Christ surpasses all, and is greater than our sins, even if we cannot sense so. We return to the conviction that if we cannot presently intuitively feel how much worthier Christ is than our sinful desires and how surpassingly beautiful is knowing Christ in us through the Holy Spirit, we trust these are true.

We do not need to feel Him to trust the God who is really there. We trust that God is who He says He is: deserving of our obedience and reverence and promising of an eternal love for us through Jesus Christ. Jude encourages: "keep yourselves in the love of God" (Jude 21a). So, we flee *aselgeia*! And we flee in faith to Christ.

In day 2 this week, we will study Jude's metaphors and analogies concerning sensuality/licentiousness. In days 3 and 4, we will study Sodom and Gomorrah and Baalam's error respectively. For today's study questions, we will consider many of Jude's explanations and descriptions concerning licentiousness (according to the chart above).

....

FOR STUDY *and* REFLECTION

....

Read Jude 4, Hebrews 11:1, and Jude 21. As you consider licentiousness, or sensuality in Jude—in its full description, including self-indulgence, greed, and sexual sin—is your heart burning about any step of faith you need to take in obedience?

Do you carry any itching desire that needs to be replaced by faith in Christ's superior worth and beauty?

Compose a prayer of confession and faith on the basis of God's supremacy, majesty, and mercy.

Complete the chart below to study Jude's explanations and descriptions concerning licentiousness/sensuality.

Jude's Explanations and Descriptions for Irreverence

JUDE'S DESCRIPTION OF INTERLOPERS	NOTES AND CROSS REFERENCES:	HOW CAN I BE OPPOSITE OF THE INTERLOPERS?
"Relying on their dreams, [they] defile the flesh" (v. 8)	"What the reference to these people as 'dreamers' means is that these individuals were claiming divine revelation as the basis of their practices,"[9] but all prophecy must be based on the faith, not special knowledge outside of God's revelation (see Jude 3).	
"But these people blaspheme all that they do not understand, and they are destroyed by all that they, like unreasoning animals, understand instinctively" (v. 10)	"The natural person does not accept the things of the Spirit of God, for they are folly to him, and he is not able to understand them because they are spiritually discerned" (1 Cor. 2:14). "Their end is destruction, their god is their belly, and they glory in their shame, with minds set on earthly things" (Phil. 3:19).	
"Following their own sinful desires . . . showing favoritism to gain advantage" (v. 16)	"For, speaking loud boasts of folly, they entice by sensual passions of the flesh those who are barely escaping from those who live in error" (2 Peter 2:18).	
"Worldly people" (v. 19)	"Do not love the world or the things in the world. If anyone loves the world, the love of the Father is not in him. For all that is in the world—the desires of the flesh and the desires of the eyes and pride of life—is not from the Father but is from the world" (1 John 2:15–16).	

WEEK 5 | DAY 2

For certain people have crept in unnoticed who long ago were designated for this condemnation, ungodly people, who pervert the grace of our God into sensuality and deny our only Master and Lord, Jesus Christ.

JUDE 4

Cross reference: *Claiming to be wise, they became fools, and exchanged the glory of the immortal God for images resembling mortal man and birds and animals and creeping things. Therefore God gave them up in the lusts of their hearts to impurity, to the dishonoring of their bodies among themselves, because they exchanged the truth about God for a lie and worshiped and served the creature rather than the Creator, who is blessed forever! Amen.*

ROMANS 1:22–25

Father, Your wrath is revealed from heaven against all ungodliness and unrighteousness of men, who by their unrighteousness suppress the truth. Let my heart submit to You. You are blessed forever. Amen.

EXCHANGING LICENTIOUSNESS FOR TRUTH

When lusting, acting on instinct, being carried along by desire, or acting wildly and being uprooted, clear thinking becomes obscured by desire. Jude indicates so. In yesterday's study questions, we examined the interlopers Jude describes as "unreasoning animals" (v. 10). Once we have a reasoned understanding of the gospel, as we have noted in this week's introduction, the contradiction between God's holy love and a sense of license to lust, greed, and indulgence becomes abundantly apparent. We need clear thinking.

While putting human reason above the Scriptures is contrary to the authority of the Bible, the Bible teaches a right place for reason. Some might question why we see Jude disparage those who would abandon logic, while Christianity is concerned with having faith. And indeed in the previous lesson, we looked at faith as a response to ungodly passions and licentiousness. How, some might ask, can the Bible teach us to not be unreasoning, and simultaneously to have faith? In response: a biblical faith does not constitute an irrational leap—as if Christianity requires blindness to reason the same way that following unbridled sinful desires produces a blindness to reason.

Carl F. H. Henry, a twentieth-century theologian, writes that faith in "certain basic truths does not at all require a dismissal of reason and evidence to authentic faith."[10] Instead, he teaches that the Christian faith is reasonable, and that the Bible's logical validity attests to this fact. Therefore, he cites words of Augustine: *credo ut intelligam*—"I believe in order to understand."[11] The woman of faith readily acknowledges that there is much she does not know, and she accepts God's Word to be God's by faith; however, with the same breath, she confesses that the Bible she accepts by faith is coherent, that by studying it her understanding increases, and that the God she meets through its words springs forth truth.

Our reasoning minds submit to Scripture with faith, and then the God of our Scriptures leads us to a faith that is logical. Henry, therefore, warns us against a conversion to Christianity as merely "an exchange of one set of feelings for another"[12]—worldly feelings for feelings about Jesus. Were our feelings about Jesus or about our religious experiences the basis of our truth affirmations, we could easily licentiously surmise that our own fulfillment is Jesus' highest value: "Jesus is good and for me. This [pleasurable sin, worldly philosophy, etc.] makes me feel fulfilled, so Jesus would want this for me." We might even sense intuitively this type of false "freedom" in our intuitions as being from God.

With this mindset, searching the Scriptures and studying them for what God has actually breathed out for us to know seems scarcely needed. Instead of submitting ourselves to God and His Word, a supposed feeling of God can deceive us. How misleading our intuitions can prove to be! How they tempt us to exchange clear scriptural truth about God for a lie and worship and serve the creature's perceptions rather than the Creator (Rom. 1:25)!

FOR STUDY *and* REFLECTION

Read Romans 1:18–25. How are exchanging God's glory for earthly images and God's truth for a lie capable of blinding people to sin?

Reflect on and write down why the Christian faith is not irrational. List some reasons you know from Scripture that God is logical. Also list some of what you have come to understand more clearly about yourself and/or the world through studying Scripture that you could have known no other way.

In what ways does the reasonableness of the faith not equate to human reason being elevated above Scripture?

According to Romans 1:22, those swayed by worldly mindsets claim to be wise but become fools. As a Christian, consider the opposite: How has admitting your foolishness in and of yourself before God ushered you into wisdom?

Complete the chart below to study Jude's metaphors and analogies concerning licentiousness/sensuality.

Jude's Metaphors and Analogies for Irreverence

JUDE'S DESCRIPTION OF INTERLOPERS	NOTES AND CROSS REFERENCES:	HOW CAN I BE OPPOSITE OF THE INTERLOPERS?
"Shepherds feeding themselves" (v. 12)	"Ah, shepherds of Israel who have been feeding yourselves! Should not shepherds feed the sheep?" (Ezek. 34:2b)	
"Waterless clouds, swept along by winds" (v. 12)	"Like clouds and wind without rain is a man who boasts of a gift he does not give" (Prov. 25:14). "The term translated without water (*anudros*) also occurs in Matthew 12:43 in reference to the wanderings of evil spirits through dry and barren places (cf. Luke 11:24–26). By describing false teachers in the same way that Luke describes demons, Jude reiterated the connection between the apostates and their satanic sources."[13]	
"Fruitless trees in late autumn, twice dead" (v. 12)	"You will recognize them by their fruits. Are grapes gathered from thornbushes, or figs from thistles?" (Matt. 7:16). "Autumn is the season when farmers and gardeners expect to harvest the final crops of the year. If nothing comes, they must endure disappointment and hardship through the winter. The next spring they can begin again the painstaking process of fertilizing, planting, watering, and waiting for the crop to mature. With this in mind, the phrase **autumn trees without fruit** pictures the disappointing reality of a barren harvest. Jude likened the apostates' empty profession and utter lack of spiritual life to a barren harvest. He called them **doubly dead;** first, they are fruitless because there is no life in them; second, they are **uprooted**, dead at the very core."[14]	

*. . . just as Sodom and Gomorrah and the sur-
rounding cities, which likewise indulged in sexual
immorality and pursued unnatural desire, serve
as an example by undergoing a punishment of
eternal fire.*
JUDE 7

Cross reference: *Read Genesis 19:1–22.*

*God, You are my Creator. You have made me for loving obedience of You. Thank You for
designing me and giving me commands that help me know who You are and how I can
reflect You.*

SEXUAL IMMORALITY AND UNNATURAL DESIRE

One lie of this age is that if our feelings are perceivably guided and steered, they
are no longer genuine. The message is something like, "We must feel what we feel,
and in order to be ourselves, we must live out whatever we feel." But Jude teaches
that if we do not apply understanding and reason to our feelings, then our feelings
will ultimately destroy us: "they [the interlopers] are destroyed by all that they, like

unreasoning animals, understand instinctively" (v. 10). One fundamental belief of Christianity is that when we were separated from God through the fall of Adam and Eve, we were separated by sin from being all that God created us to be. So, Christianity claims the opposite of the world: we can have true authenticity, to be who we were created to be, only when in pure fellowship with the God who designed us. That is our great hope, a precious aim here on earth and a joyous expectation to be fully realized in future glory.

Yet, Jude brings us another serious warning that even authenticity cannot be our ultimate goal. Authenticity to being the creations God intended for us to be is a byproduct of obeying Him as our Lord. For not only are we inauthentic if we choose another way than God's, revealed according to Scripture, if we choose our own way, we declare ourselves to be "god."

But for God to be God, as He is, there can only be One. Reject Him within this broad present time of mercy and grace for receiving Him and, reminds Jude, wrath will come.

Charles Spurgeon describes the scenes at Sodom and Gomorrah:

> The cities of Sodom and Gomorrah are bright as the sun goes down. The inhabitants are merry with boisterous laughter. There is plenty in the barn. There is luxury in the hall, for the plain of Sodom was well watered and lacked for nothing. Down went that sun upon a disastrous evening—never to rise upon the most of those who were in that doomed city. At daybreak, just as the sun is beginning to shine upon the earth, angels had hastened Lot and his family out of the city—and no sooner had they reached the little city of Zoar than straightway the Heaven is red with supernatural flame and down descends a terrific rain—as if God had poured Hell out of Heaven! He rained fire and brimstone upon the cities and the smoke of their torment went up so that Abraham, far away to the west, could see the rolling cloud and the terrible brightness of the fire, even at midday.

And as men go to the "Lacus Asphaltites," or the Dead Sea, they see to this day where death has reigned. There are masses of asphalt still floating upon the surface of that sea where there is nothing that lives. No fish swim in its turbid streams. There are indubitable evidences there of some dread judgment of God. And as Jude thought of this, he seemed to say, "Oh God, preserve us from such a doom, for this is the doom of all apostates, either in this world, or in that which is to come, thus to be consumed with fire."[15]

Sodom was rife with sensuality; Jude says that they "indulged in sexual immorality and pursued unnatural desire" (Jude 7). They clearly did not adhere to the biblical standard and gift of sexual intimacy being reserved for lifelong marriage between a man and a woman. The widely held interpretation that the sins of Sodom included homosexuality is the natural and historic understanding.[16]

A life of complacency, plenty, and selfishness characterized Sodom and, according to Ezekiel 16:48–50, this led these men to elevate their own desires and commit sexual "abomination" (Ezek. 16:50) before the Lord. They became a group mastered by their desires, enslaved to them. To communicate God's wrath and judgment for sin with those caught up in such things is to lovingly warn them; we don't speak these truths because we take pleasure in the destruction of people—never (Ezek. 33:11). Rather, we can speak of wrath because it is a reality.

As we do, we must be willing to bear the label of being judgmental; it's not a new accusation. Lot was not the light and witness for God he could have been to Sodom, and even still, the people thought he was judgmental toward them according to Genesis 19:9. Unscriptural judgment of others looks like elevating self, ignoring personal sin, forgetting one's personal need for mercy, diminishing others, and viewing others primarily in terms of their sins (Matt. 7:1–6).

Further unscriptural judgment of unbelievers means forgetting as we interact with them that they do not have a spiritual understanding of the Word or the indwelling of the Spirit we all so desperately need to guide us (1 Cor. 5:12). But speaking God's truth that can lift a person to Him, help a person be authentically who he or she was created to be, and *prevent* his or her judgment is not judgmental—even when it does offend another's desire to be god of his or her own life.

In all sexual immorality and unnatural desire, hope is not found in searching our own desires, but in adopting the truth as our own highest way. At a peak of holy love in his letter,[17] Jude proclaims not hopelessness but the hope of a reasoned, committed repentance.

For Study *and* Reflection

Refer to Jude 7 and read Ephesians 5:3. What are some "new" descriptions of sexual morality popular today? How can we react to these redefinitions of God's design for the gift of sexuality?

According to Ephesians 5:3, to what standard of holiness are believers called by God?

Refer to Genesis 19:1–22 and 2 Peter 2:6–8 and note Lot's actions and characteristics. Why can you be reassured that God's mercy comes to sinners?

What is the difference between Lot and the people of Sodom, that he and his family were provided escape?

Have you ever been called judgmental by an unbeliever? Was he or she right or wrong?

Read Jude 23. According to Galatians 6:1 and 3, what healthy fear is Jude likely admonishing the recipients to have?

Read Jude 10, 23, and 2 Peter 2:19. How can understanding these verses together help you engage those who want to turn from sexual immorality and unnatural desire?

Refer back to Zechariah 3:1–5 and note the similarities with Jude 23. In Christ, how are mercy and truth both upheld?

WEEK 5 | DAY 4

*Woe to them! For they . . . abandoned themselves
for the sake of gain to Balaam's error . . .*
JUDE 11

Cross reference: *Forsaking the right way, they have gone astray. They
have followed the way of Balaam, the son of Beor, who loved gain from
wrongdoing, but was rebuked for his own transgression; a speechless
donkey spoke with human voice and restrained the prophet's madness.*
2 PETER 2:15–16

*Father, please make me aware of what most influences my heart as it relates to money.
Show me any thanklessness and greed that I maintain. You are my greatest gain, my
greatest treasure; in Christ, I am rich.*

GREED

According to Numbers 22–24, Balaam refused an offer from Balak, the Moabite
king, to put a curse on the Israelites for monetary gain—a good choice. However,
according to Numbers 31:16, Balaam ultimately seduced Israel to sexual immorality and idolatry, specifically, the worship of Baal (see also Num. 25:1–3). He also
intended to curse Israel (Deut. 23:3–6; Josh. 24:9–10; Neh. 13:2). Despite being

rebuked by a donkey, confronted by the Lord, and uttering a messianic prophecy (Num. 24:17), Balaam loved the financial gain that could come from enacting evil spiritual influence (2 Peter 2:15–16).

Balak was worried that the Israelites would destroy his kingdom of Moab, as they had the Amorites. Some of the Amorites' sin had reached its full measure (cf. Gen. 15:16), given that two Amorite kings were defeated (Num. 21).[18] Therefore, God—the just Judge of all the earth (Gen. 18:25)—had determined for the Amorites to be judged. Balaam's advice to nearby Balak, therefore, was ultimately to conspire to put a "stumbling block" in the way of the Israelites to entice them to sin (Rev. 2:14). It was a devious idea. If only Balak's concern had led him to repent of immorality and idolatry, and lead his people humbly toward reverent fear of the Lord who has authority over soul and body! But instead, fear mixed with his pride, and he crafted a plan to prevent earthly destruction.

For his part, Balaam had only thought of the money that he might gain by participating in this scheme. Jude, however, writes in verse 11 that, like Balaam, the false teachers, for the sake of gain, "abandon themselves"—meaning, they pour themselves out (Greek *ekcheo*). Instead of any true gain, Balaam and the interlopers lose themselves to greed.

For Study *and* Reflection

Read Numbers 22, 2 Peter 2:15–16, and Revelation 2:14. What opportunities did Balaam have to genuinely follow the Lord with faith, devotion, and love?

How is merely restraining oneself from sin different from following the Lord?

What desires pulled at both Balaam and Balak?

According to 2 Peter 2:15–16 and Revelation 2:14, what were the motives and actions that characterized Balaam's heart?

How do these men demonstrate the difficulty of seeing past the pervasive desires of the human heart?

What are the strongest desires pulling at your heart?

According to Genesis 15:16, why is God's judgment measured and deliberate?

According to the sins of Moab listed in Numbers 25:1–3, describe the justice of God's judgment.

Read Jude 11 and 2 Corinthians 8:9. Reflect on how and why we lose ourselves if we do not follow in the ways of the Lord.

Do you ever believe you will gain more by following ungodly desires instead of the Lord's will?

Do you consider yourself already wealthy because you know Christ? Compose a prayer of thanks to Him.

WEEK 5 | DAY 5

May mercy, peace, and love be multiplied to you.
JUDE 2

"She Looks to the Sky" *by Sherri Youngward*

They say she is loved by the greatest of all
Who have walked in the world
He lives far away, still she spends all her days
Content with only His words

She often walks alone, but never is she
    lonely
You can offer her anything
Her affections are all for Him only

She looks to the sky
As if He is coming down through the
    clouds up above
Though no one has seen Him you cannot
    deny
She is drenched with His love

She often walks alone, but never is she
    lonely
You can offer her anything
Her affections are all for Him only

All the day long she sings sweetly
She says He speaks to her mind
She's only rich with affliction
Yet a bitter word you won't find

She lives with assurance He loves her too
    deeply
To let such distance remain
She's brimming with longing for Him to
    come calling
And sweep her away.[19]

LOVE MULTIPLIED

When tempted to lusts that seem to pull us like wild waves into the sea, we can return to faith (week 5, day 1). Faith births the boldness to say, "I trust God is greater than this temptation, though I do not see or sense it at this moment." Hope follows, saying, "One day, I will hate this sin as fully as I should. One day, this temptation, this sin, will mean nothing to me." Love is the greatest: "How I do love my Lord more and desire Him first, and all accords with who He is!"

As a Christian student in public school, I often refrained from various activities and conversations of my peers. I am thankful for wonderful friendships in my school years. But I also remember returning home in the evenings and listening to Sherri Youngward's song quoted above. I was particularly attuned to: "She often walks alone, but never is she lonely. You can offer her anything. Her affections are all for Him only." These words resonated with me, for walking alone through my school halls was not lonely; I already had Christ. Years later, in seminary, I was drawn to the writings of Jonathan Edwards, an eighteenth-century pastor/theologian. When I took a class on his theology, his list of resolutions to live for God in view of the brevity of days on earth was especially instructive. Imagine my joy on discovering how Sherri Youngward's song and the theologian's writings intertwine: Youngward based her verses on Edwards's reflections about his love interest! In 1723, Jonathan Edwards wrote these lyrical words of admiration for Sarah Pierrepont, who would become his wife:

> They say there is a young lady in [New-Haven] who is loved of that Great Being, who made and rules the world, and that there are certain seasons in which this Great Being, in some way or other invisible, comes to her and fills her mind with exceeding sweet delight; and that she hardly cares for any thing, except to meditate on him—that she expects after a while to be received up where he is, to be raised up out of the world and caught up into heaven; being assured that he loves her too well to let her remain at a distance from him always. There she is to dwell with him, and to be ravished with his love and delight for ever. Therefore, if you present all the world before her, with the

richest of its treasures, she disregards it and cares not for it, and is unmindful of any pain or affliction. She has a strange sweetness in her mind, and singular purity in her affections; is most just and conscientious in all her conduct; and you could not persuade her to do any thing wrong or sinful, if you would give her all the world, lest she should offend this Great Being. She is of a wonderful sweetness, calmness, and universal benevolence of mind; especially after this Great God has manifested himself to her mind. She will sometimes go about from place to place, singing sweetly; and seems to be always full of joy and pleasure; and no one knows for what. She loves to be alone, walking in the fields and groves, and seems to have some one invisible always conversing with her.[20]

Knowing whose writing inspired Youngward's song gave me a new dimension of appreciation for it. One resolution of Edwards was "to study the Scriptures so steadily, constantly, and frequently, as that I may find, and plainly perceive, myself to grow in the knowledge of the same."[21] Scripture is the foundation of what he esteemed in Sarah Pierrepont. Seeming to reflect his own heart toward Scripture, ever before her mind were truths of God. Edwards noted admiringly, "she hardly cares for any thing, except to meditate on him."[22] Youngward reflects this in her song, writing that Pierrepont was "content with only His words."[23] We see, therefore, in Pierrepont an example of someone who, through building herself up in the faith in accordance with Scripture, kept herself consistently in the love of God (Jude 20–21).

Paul wrote about Christ's love in the believer's life: "For the love of Christ controls us, because we have concluded this: that one has died for all, therefore all have died; and he died for all, that those who live might no longer live for themselves but for him who for their sake died and was raised" (2 Cor. 5:14–15). The sacrificial love of Christ "controls," wrote Paul.

The Greek word used here for "controls" evokes the idea of urging on, impelling, totally dominating. One commentator concludes, then, "Christ's love is a compulsive force in the life of believers, a dominating power that effectively eradicates choice in that it leaves them no option but to live for God."[24] May we all have such love for God!

As we learned in week 1, day 3, we who believe are called to be slaves of Christ, and the substance of our being driven to this servitude is love for God in response to the love Christ has shown to us.

Edwards observed how this manner of love of the holy overtakes Pierrepont, producing a life with "singular purity in her affections . . . you could not persuade her to do any thing wrong or sinful, if you would give her all the world, lest she should offend this Great Being."[25] Love obeys, just as the Lord said (John 14:15)—when well-understood, this is what God's loving graciousness works within us.

For Study *and* Reflection

Read through the epistle of Jude and note every instance of "beloved" or "love."

Reflect on whether or not any notion or belief you possess might try to dissuade you from being convinced that you are beloved of God.

Seek to follow the example of Jonathan Edwards: "*Resolved*, To examine carefully and constantly, what that one thing in me is, which causes me in the least to doubt of the love of God; and so direct all my forces against it."[26] What are some practical ways you can do this? For example, you might make a list of your own resolutions to revisit again and again; you might identify a fellow church member to imitate in Christlikeness and grow to become better acquainted with this person.

John reminds us that "God is light" and "God is love" (1 John 1:5; 4:8). Since both are true, describe why love and licentiousness are incompatible—and why hell is necessary.

How can you be watchful for any tendencies to make grace a reason to sin instead of a reason to obey?

How is negating God's light to diminish God's love?

Read 2 Corinthians 5:11, 14–15, 18–20. Knowing the fear of the Lord and being controlled by Christ's love, how can you follow Paul's example? What is the message that must be shared?

See 2 Corinthians 5:19 and 21. What is not held against you, and what have you become?

How do these truths help you understand what it means to be controlled by Christ's love?

Why can we not be controlled by Christ's love without righteousness? How does righteousness enable love to be multiplied?

He Is Able to Keep Us

I wonder if Jude's conclusion to his letter might surprise some. In his brief writing, he does not instruct his recipients as to the mechanics of how they would confront the false teachers—surely some purposeful meetings and actions would need to occur. But at the end of a series of warnings, Jude directs hearts and minds to the God who is with the church as growth happens.

Remember what you have been taught by the apostles, who were with the Lord, Jude instructs. *Build yourself up in Him through the faith*, is the sense of his instructions. *Set your hearts on mercy, the mercy you who believe are set to receive in place of judgment, and that you are therefore equipped to demonstrate to others.*

He lifts their hearts and minds to the holiness of their calling as beloved of Jesus Christ; he reminds them of what world and self can never give—eternal, sweet, magnificent, unparalleled fellowship with God. That is precious.

As I never want to see my little daughter plunge down a staircase, Jude reminds his recipients of the preciousness of their fellowship with God so that they would fully share in desiring to maintain a faith not bruised, cut, or displaced. He asks that they share in protecting what is dear, staying together in all that is true as Christ's beloved people. And how joyful it is for a church to celebrate with each person who—when false teaching has been unveiled—chooses to remain faithful and move in unison with the teaching once-delivered and compassionately help others do the same.

"I have kept the faith," Paul wrote to Timothy (2 Tim. 4:7). This is the same Paul who confessed in Romans 7:15, "For what I want to do I do not do, but what I hate I do" (NIV). Keeping the faith, then, does not consist of sinless perfection, but the adherence to believing what has been taught as the unalterable truth and aim. The truth may be clarified, but it is never improved upon. It may be given more precise descriptions by theologians or words better suited to each generation over time, but it does not change. "I have kept the faith" involves that our priorities concerning truth, godly aims concerning sin, and our fundamental beliefs are unshifting, even as we change.

We may do what we do not *want* to do; we may not do as we would have dearly *liked* to have done—and yet, in seeking to keep the faith, those likes and wants remain intact (or are improved with knowledge of Scripture). All that Jesus Christ loves—anything we could be convinced from His Word He loves—we desire to hear, love, believe, cherish, do, follow, and obey.

And in all He hates, we would want to conform in kind. Of course, none of this is done without fault—to believe we are without sin would be a lie (1 John 1:8). Yet, that we not lower our standards or beliefs when we or those we observe or know fail to live in accordance with Scripture is part of God's holy grace for making us like Christ through an objective revelation.

We can hate the stain of sin, even while acknowledging our ongoing personal need for mercy and lifting each other in our church contexts to truth beyond ourselves. We may confess sins to each other, when appropriate, helpful, and fitting; we may discuss the sorrows of living in a fallen world—but this is not the basis or substance of our Christ-bought commonality.

As the small church plant my husband and I attended united around each new believer's baptism and profession of personal faith in the faith, Christ's own people always unify on what is fixed: the faith and the sincere commitment we have made to seeking to know and follow Scripture as knowing and following Christ. So, Jude addresses his recipients as one—the true church. Jude's believing recipients may need to take action in separating themselves from the false teachers who once partook of the Lord's Supper with them, and at times it may have involved a sense of loneliness due to all who do not respond well. But in this world, or the next, these recipients would never be alone—and so with us.

WEEK 6 | DAY 1

But you must remember, beloved, the predictions of the apostles of our Lord Jesus Christ. They said to you, "In the last time there will be scoffers, following their own ungodly passions." It is these who cause divisions, worldly people, devoid of the Spirit.

JUDE 17–19

Cross reference: *Therefore, knowing the fear of the Lord, we persuade others.*

2 CORINTHIANS 5:11a

Father, I pray that my heart, mind, and will would be convinced of Your truth. Help me recall all that You are teaching me through the God-breathed words of Jude's epistle.

BEING PERSUADED

In verse 3, Jude calls his recipients to "contend for the faith that was once for all delivered to the saints," and in verses 17–19, Jude reminds his beloved recipients that the same apostles who had taught them the faith had also already warned them about the very kind of people Jude was condemning. Once again, Jude clarifies that he has not been the one adding to the faith—rather, the interlopers have dangerously done so.

Thomas Oden, a theologian of the twentieth century, wrote:

> No concept was more deplored by the early ecumenical councils than the notion that theology's task was to "innovate" (*neoterizein*). That implied some imagined creative addition to the apostolic teaching and thus something "other than" (*heteros*) the received doctrine (*doxa*), "the baptism into which we have been baptized." What the ancient church teachers *least* wished for a theology was that it would be "fresh" or "self-expressive" or an embellishment of purely private inspirations, as if these might stand as some "decisive improvement" on the apostolic teaching.[1]

I could imagine Jude hoped that others would say that he invented no new doctrine. Jude's letter had not been a matter of his own opinions or theological innovations, but a defense of the church against novel teachings—additions to the apostolic understanding of the faith—that had been influencing his recipients. Because of this, he could confidently say that not he, but the interlopers, were causing the divisions.

Jude's letter does not provide an opportunity in which two sides present arguments and then compromise between the two parties should occur so that all can move forward to other church business. No compromise with lawlessness, irreverence, and licentiousness should be made. No compromise with sins of the soul, spirit, and body should be abided. No compromises concerning the authority, worthiness, and holiness of God should be permitted. And persistent, unrepentant church members who are causing others to compromise with false doctrine, pursue compromise with sin, and enjoy compromise concerning an understanding of God's character should not be tolerated.

Last week, in day 5, we looked at 2 Corinthians 5, when Paul wrote about persuading others (v. 11). One analysis of Jude by F. Duane Watson has seen this letter as using an ancient rhetoric form for its structure, a deliberative rhetoric that "places attention on persuasion."[2] It is interesting to examine how scholars Douglas Moo[3] and Peter Davids[4] describe the structure of Jude. Combining various areas of the outlines they each define, the outline of the epistle would be as follows. You might want to read through Jude as you look at this outline below.

Verses 1–2 are the *epistolary prescript*.

Verse 3 is the *exordium*, the purpose statement that introduces the writer's main argument. Jude is asking readers to contend for the faith.

Verse 4 is the *narratio*, in which shared assumptions are established—the grace of *our* God is being perverted, and Jesus Christ as *our* Master and Lord is being denied. This section also introduces the reason or occasion for the writing—in this case, the "certain people" who have "crept in unnoticed."

Verses 5–16 comprise the *probatio*, which gives arguments and proofs for the purpose of persuasion. Jude seeks to contrast the interlopers' understandings of Christ with the implicit true faith the recipients had already received, and to promote the urgency of contending for the true faith by demonstrating and describing the interlopers' errors and outcomes.

Verses 17–23 comprise the *peroratio*, which "repeats the case and appeals to the emotions."[5] In verses 17–19 Jude repeats the basics of the interlopers' error and a proper dependency upon the apostles' teaching.

Jude ends with doxology in verses 24–25.

In stating in verse 19 that the interlopers are devoid of the Holy Spirit, Jude puts the final stamp of disapproval on these false teachers. Should any want to toy with their teaching or entertain it, Jude concludes that these are "earthly people who are not governed by the Spirit."[6] As with Jude's original readers, we can know that Scripture has been given to persuade us on the unalterable faith passed to us—so, may we be entirely persuaded.

For Study *and* Reflection

Considering Jude's recipients had not addressed the errors of the false teachers (vv. 4, 12), why might some be tempted to see Jude as the one causing divisions?

According to Jude 17–19, Jude is adamant about the opposite. Why? How could his recipients know Jude was not the one in error?

How can we tell the difference today between those who are causing divisions and those who are addressing false teaching that divides people from the truth?

According to verses 17–19, Jude determines to refer to the apostolic authority from which his recipients had first heard their doctrinal teaching of the faith. Why is keeping yourself in the faith essential to following Jesus?

Has your understanding of this grown through studying Jude? What have you become persuaded of through Jude's letter?

WEEK 6 | DAY 2

But you, beloved, building yourselves up in your most holy faith and praying in the Holy Spirit, keep yourselves in the love of God, waiting for the mercy of our Lord Jesus Christ that leads to eternal life. And have mercy on those who doubt; save others by snatching them out of the fire; to others show mercy with fear, hating even the garment stained by the flesh.

JUDE 20–23

Cross reference: *His divine power has granted to us all things that pertain to life and godliness, through the knowledge of him who called us to his own glory and excellence . . .*

2 PETER 1:3

Father, I have immense gratitude for all who have helped me learn Your Word and grow in knowing and understanding what You have revealed. I pray that in my knowledge of You, I would always be fruitful and effective.

KEEPING OURSELVES, SERVING EACH OTHER

In day 1 of this week, we learned about the possible rhetorical structure in Jude for persuasion. Not only does this letter seek to convince, it takes the further step of asking "readers to make decisions on a course of action with reference to the future."[7] Jude intends for his teaching, warnings, and reminders to produce deeds on the part of his recipients of a specific nature that involves all the steps in verses 20–23: building up in faith, praying in the Holy Spirit, keeping within God's love, living in the hope of God's mercy, and deliberately helping others in mercy and purity.

Increased scriptural knowledge and understanding of God's judgment can tempt to the opposite types of responses, such as wavering from the faith, being abrasive and impatient with those possessing lesser understanding, becoming haughty or self-exalting in communications, or becoming complacent in existing knowledge. The apostle Peter's material found in 2 Peter very closely parallels Jude. But Peter includes a lengthier introduction to his letter. He shares Jude's conviction for competency in and contending for Christian knowledge when writing to fellow believers who have "obtained *a faith* of equal standing with ours" (2 Peter 1:1, emphasis added; see also 2 Peter 1:16–21). Peter is instructive regarding Christian knowledge and how to add more to one's life well.

He affirms the need for knowledge: "May grace and peace be multiplied to you in the *knowledge* of God and of Jesus our Lord" (2 Peter 1:2, emphasis added; see also v. 3). But he seeks to address the concern of being "ineffective or unfruitful in the *knowledge* of our Lord Jesus Christ" (1:8, emphasis added). Wanting to grow in the knowledge of God, we are instructed to grow well. Peter lists the following ways: "make every effort to supplement your faith with virtue, and virtue with knowledge, and knowledge with self-control, and self-control with steadfastness, and steadfastness with godliness, and godliness with brotherly affection, and brotherly affection with love" (2 Peter 1:5–7). With this in mind,

We seek to live according to the way Jesus would have for us.

We add knowledge to our knowledge.

We seek to be self-controlled in how we share and implement that knowledge in service of others.

We remain steadfast even through our exposure to new thoughts and ideas.

We determine to be devoted to God when our minds are challenged.

We interact with our brothers and sisters in Christ with genuine affection (even when others are incorrect—Jude provides an excellent example).

We seek in love to determine what will most help others come to know greater truth.

As we grow in the knowledge of God, Jude clarifies the necessity of not only working to keep ourselves, but also looking to keep others. Moo summarizes: "Withdrawal into their own private spirituality is not enough; Jude's readers must do what they can to reclaim these people before it is too late."[8] Jude works through his words to convince recipients to commit to these actions.

FOR STUDY *and* REFLECTION

"Knowledge" is mentioned in the opening of 2 Peter. Note also the openings of the following epistles, and the references to knowledge: Philippians 1:9, Colossians 1:9–10, and Ephesians 1:17. Describe the importance of scriptural knowledge based on these verses.

Read 2 Peter 1:5–7.

Make a list of every instruction to pursue in these verses.

Ask yourself: *As my knowledge of the faith grows, am I lacking in any of these areas in a way that is making me ineffective or unfruitful?*

Read 2 Peter 1:10–11. What assurance does Peter give in these verses?

Believers' actions are to be a response to what is true about the Lord (cf. 1 Cor. 10:1). Therefore, summarize truths about Him evident in Jude 20–23.

Because the faith of the Lord is something I can build my life on, that means God is: _____(v. 20).

Because I can pray in the Holy Spirit, according to Christ's truth and grace, God is: _____(v. 20).

Because the love of the Lord keeps me secure, that means God is: _____(v. 21).

Because the Lord's mercy leads to eternal life, that means God is: _____(v. 21).

Because I am taught to show mercy to those who doubt, that means God is: _____(v. 22).

Because I am taught to snatch others from the fire, that means God is: _____(v. 23).

Because I am taught to hate sin, that means God is: _____(v. 23).

Are you tempted to keep your faith private? How does being faithful to others according to Jude 20–23 reflect God's actions toward you?

WEEK 6 | DAY 3

Now to him who is able to keep you from stumbling . . .

JUDE 24a

Cross reference: *He came to his own, and his own people did not receive him. But to all who did receive him, who believed in his name, he gave the right to become children of God, who were born, not of blood nor of the will of the flesh nor of the will of man, but of God.*

JOHN 1:11–13

Father, You are just and holy. You also are both able and willing to save me. What comfort and hope! I turn toward You in my spirit and, setting You always before me, I humbly honor the sacrifice of Christ.

ABLE TO KEEP

Jude's doxology, a "brief formula for expressing praise or glory to God,"[9] begins with "now to him who is able to keep you from stumbling." While believers are instructed by Jude in verse 23 to have a healthy fear of sin when showing others mercy, Jude now reassures his recipients. Attention shifts. The same God who prescribes condemnation for false teachers is also able to keep the recipients from stumbling, or falling.[10]

For a time during Bible college, I felt overcome with my lack of faith in Christ. The second floor of my dorm building offered a private prayer room that any of the women could use—I would go within to question myself and, alone with God, I felt no assurance of my salvation. *How do I know if I am really His—that there is not some further experience of Christian belief and faith that I don't even know how to have?*

I remembered some advice from years past—whose source I have long forgotten— that you should always have, at the very least, one other committed Christian who knows the worst about you. So I forced myself to tell other people. "Dear Lianna, you *are* a Christian," they might have said in various, compassionate forms. But I was not at all sure. They pointed to Christian fruit in my life.

But I could always think of a reason I did something they considered "good" for myself and not for God. How did I know that the faith I had was truly saving faith? It surely did not feel like faith worthy of a great, all-powerful, all-knowing, holy, and majestic God far beyond my understanding. How could I know that I knew Him and that, in the end, I would persevere? How did I know that I had adequately confessed my sin? The wrong motives that seeped through everything I did were an unspeakable burden.

One morning, the school president concluded his chapel message by saying that he kept a list in the back of his Bible of names of those who had fallen away from the faith—as a reminder to himself to stay true to Christ, the gospel, and a high view of all of Scripture. And then he said that he would not presume there would not be any, even in an audience of all Bible school students, who felt they were not sure they knew Christ. That was me—I did not feel sure! How did I know I would not one day find my name on such a list as he kept?

Not many days later, I sat in a theology professor's office, and he asked, "What do you want to talk about today?"

"Well, I guess I really don't know if I'm a Christian," I admitted, my heart sinking at the audible admission. I wanted him to reply with an answer telling me that if I felt a certain way or had gone through a certain experience, then I was "in," or "okay."

He looked straight at me, "Let me ask you this: Do you believe that Christ is strong enough to save you?"

"I think so." It was a sincere answer, but I also honestly believed that this was beside the point. I rephrased for his benefit. "But how do I know if *I* have really believed well enough in Him?"

He told me I had the wrong starting point and went on to encourage me that if I thought Christ strong enough to save, to then join with the man in Mark 9:24 who prayed, "I believe; help my unbelief!" concerning the rest.

He lifted me from my subjectively focused concerns, and set me on the objective revelation of Christ. Charles Spurgeon advises the same:

> A Christian has no right to be always saying—"Do I love the Lord or no? Am I His, or am I not?" He may be compelled to say it, sometimes, but it is far better for him to come just as he is and throw himself at the foot of the Cross and say, "Savior, You have promised to save those that believe! I believe, therefore You have saved me!" I know some think this is presumption, but surely it is worse than presumption not to believe God! And it is true humility to take God at His word and to believe Him.[11]

I do believe in Christ—not with the faith that God deserves, but with the faith the size of a mustard seed I have. I still ask God to help my unbelief. But my greatest confidence is that only Christ can save me, that Christ is able to save me, and that He is willing (John 1:11–13). Yes, we must repent of sin and express personal faith in Christ to be born again. But how to assure the fragile believer that he or she has truly saving faith? In Jude, the warning to spur contending for the true faith and the benediction to praise God are a unit. The truth is, Christ is able to keep His saints. And the truth is how we know.

FOR STUDY *and* REFLECTION

After reading of condemnation, judgment, and destruction—and then thinking of the mercy of God in Christ Jesus—why is turning one's thoughts to praise at the conclusion of this epistle immensely fitting?

In Jude, how do you see the warnings and the benediction as relating?

How might those in different spiritual states react to Jude's letter:

Apostates is derived from the Greek *apo* and *stenai*, meaning "off from" or "to stand away from"—i.e., rejection of the faith once professed.

Heresy (Greek *hairein*) means "to take" or "to choose"—i.e., to choose teachings for oneself that diverge from the faith delivered.

A person with heretical beliefs or a carnal Christian might:

A regular church attender who is not yet a believer might:

A devoted Christian who has been at unease about the interlopers, but unable to articulate why, might:

A doubting Christian who does not know if he or she will be saved from the wrath to come might:

What is your overall response to Jude's letter?

What confidence do you personally gain through:

Christ's ability to keep you (Jude 24a)?

God's willingness to welcome you (John 1:11–13)?

God's intentional plan of salvation (Gen. 3:15)?

WEEK 6 | DAY 4

. . . and to present you blameless before the presence of his glory with great joy. . .
JUDE 24b

Cross reference: *You make known to me the path of life; in your presence there is fullness of joy; at your right hand are pleasures forevermore.*
PSALM 16:11

Father, one day, I will be present with You in perfect holiness. Oh, how I thank You for the hope of that glorious, peace-filled day.

ABLE TO PRESENT

When Jude writes that God will present us who believe blameless, the underlying meaning is that He "'stands' us before his presence."[12] Not only will we not fall, we will be upright: "While 'present' is the better translation [in Jude 26b], the Greek reader would not miss the contrast of standing and falling. They are different aspects of the same thing: if one does not fall in the world, then one stands before God."[13]

More than saved from falling, we who believe will be upheld into glory. Scriptural doctrine reminds us that God has set Himself on this plan from the beginning.

As mentioned in week 2, day 1, in Genesis we behold the mercy of God that He did not deal with us as He could have in justice, but deferred eternal punishment for mankind. Christ came to be just and the justifier for all who would believe (Rom. 3:26).

And now, coming to Jude, we read his beautiful praise that—though we fell in sin and the world is fallen, though marks of judgment abound, the decay of the world is apparent, and the gravity of sin surrounds us and is sorrowfully found within us—Christ is able to keep us and make us stand.

Spurgeon expounds on three aspects of the believer's blamelessness, to be fully enjoyed when this life has passed:

> He will *wash us* till there is not a spot left, for the chief of sinners shall be as white and fair as God's purest angel. The eye of justice will look and God will say, No spot of sin remains in you.[14]

> If a man had no faults it would still be necessary for him to have some virtues. A man cannot enter Heaven simply because transgression is put away. The Law must be kept! There must be a positive obedience to Divine precepts. . . . Therefore *the Lord our God imputes to us the perfect Righteousness of His Son Christ Jesus*. . . . The righteousness of Jesus Christ will make the saint who wears it so fair that he will be positively faultless. Yes, perfect in the sight of God.[15]

> . . . and best, perhaps, *the Spirit of God will make new creatures of us.* He has begun the work and He will finish it. He will make us so perfectly holy that we shall have no tendency to sin any more. The day will come when we shall feel that Adam in the garden was not more pure than we are. You shall have no taint of evil in you. Judgment, memory, will—every power and passion shall be emancipated from the thralldom of evil. You shall be holy even as God is holy and in His Presence you shall dwell forever![16]

Faultlessness, righteousness, and perfect holiness forever will be received by all who believe.

Now, considering these truths about the final state of believers, we might wonder what Paul means, then, in telling Christians "we will all stand before the judgment seat of God" (Rom. 14:10), or "we must all appear before the judgment seat of Christ, so that each one may receive what is due for what he has done in the body, whether good or evil" (2 Cor. 5:10).

We might wonder: *For what judgment?* Our spotless, righteous standing is cemented through Christ, and our holy beings unable to sin will become set in glory. Yet, the topic of the good works we have actually done as followers of Christ in this life remains. This judgment of the believer—not for condemnation, but evaluation— is called the *bema* seat judgment.[17] This is not a matter of salvation, but a time when rewards will be distributed for the works that we as believers have done in this life (1 Cor. 3:10–15; Eph. 6:8).[18]

Theologian Robert Culver suggests a possible sense of regret on believers' part over "what might have been"[19] at the time of this judgment—like good works we could have performed on this earth, but neglected, or sins we could have fought with more vigor, but did not. Jonathan Edwards concludes that following this judgment of evaluation, ultimately all will be perfectly satisfied when ushered into glorious eternity, though some with more of a degree of splendor in glory—presumably based on rewards for their good works—than others (1 Cor. 15:41):

> And the apostle Paul tells us that, as one star differs from another star in glory, so also it shall be in the resurrection of the dead. 1 Cor. 15:41. [. . .] It will be no damp to the happiness of those who have lower degrees of happiness and glory, that there are others advanced in glory above them: for all shall be perfectly happy, every one shall be perfectly satisfied. Every vessel that is cast into this ocean of happiness is full, though there are some vessels far larger than others.[20]

I think of how the elders cast their crowns before the feet of the Lord (Rev. 4:10–11), perhaps crowns of their rewards. Whatever we have will certainly be perfectly offered to Him in worship. The more works that will survive into glory (1 Cor. 3:14–15), I assume the more we will have to set before His feet. And we will only be grateful for others and what they set before His feet because more and more glory ascribed to our God will be our eternal song. Christ alone is able to present us blameless—and with great joy—and we who believe will be so in the splendor of glory in the presence of the Lord (Ps. 16:11). So let us more than conquer now, for great glory then!

For Study *and* Reflection

Why can we have no less than a perfect fullness of joy in heaven? See Psalm 16:11.

Read 1 Corinthians 15:40–41. Why does the perfect fullness of joy before Christ in glory not preclude the biblical teaching of heavenly rewards?

Read 2 Corinthians 5:10–11. How do you know Paul is addressing believers in verse 10?

Read Ephesians 6:8 and 1 Corinthians 3:10–15. What do you note about the Bible's teaching on how your works here relate to glory?

Read Revelation 4:10–11. Ask yourself: *Do I live fully for Him? Might I need to renew my devotion to Christ this day?*

WEEK 6 | DAY 5

As we conclude our time in Jude, meditation on the whole of Jude's doxology seems fitting. Read and pray these words:

> Now to him who is able to keep you from stumbling
> and to present you blameless before the presence of his glory with great joy,
> to the only God, our Savior, through Jesus Christ our Lord,
> be glory, majesty, dominion, and authority, before all time and now and forever.
> Amen.
> JUDE 24–25

TO THE ONLY GOD

Heard independently of the studies we have done in Jude, the phrase "keeping the faith" might be reminiscent of a certain brand of positivity, evincing trust that people will ultimately better the world in the end, or that, despite how difficult our circumstances may be, we human beings will endure because we are resilient and powerful. How contrasting to a biblical meaning of "keeping the faith," a concept that belongs to the Bible (see 2 Tim. 4:7)!

Keeping the faith, biblically, includes believing that this world will face God's judgment for sin when He deems the time to be right—no form of betterment will prevent the Judge from coming. We draw strength from Christ to endure until He returns: "Consider him who endured such opposition from sinners, so that you will not grow weary and lose heart" (Heb. 12:3 NIV).

And, then, the faith involves our exultation that any who believe in Christ will be kept from condemnation by *His* power. For we are further sustained by the hope that He will return in glory, majesty, dominion, and authority (Jude 25). Of Jude's words of praise, Hesselgrave and Hesselgrave write:

> Praise does not add something to God. It does not make Him something that He has not already been in the past or something that He would not otherwise be in the future. Rather, praise acknowledges God to be the Person He already is and always will be. And this is incredibly important because when, in the world to come, God is God to all His creatures, *all will be well with that world.* One might say that though praise does not change God into someone He otherwise would not be or add something to God that He does not already possess, it does change *us* and it does add something to *us.* It helps change us into something we were reborn to be—Christlike persons. And it adds a dimension of life we were reborn to exhibit—triumph. The gates of hell will not prevail. Beleaguered and besieged, the Church militant will become the Church triumphant—through Jesus Christ our Lord. Amen.[21]

Not only is praise sure to be on our lips for the age to come, but let it be now too. For this thought can be recovered: *keep the faith.*

Keep the faith of propositional, biblical truth being core since Christianity does not reduce to a feeling, but pinnacles around a Person whom we can know.

Keep the faith that soul, spirit, and body can be freed from worldly darkness to worship the Creator.

Keep the faith that His mercy, peace, and love mean that a perfect God is taking needy, lost people and calling us what we could never be without Him.

Keep the faith that bows us in submission, reverence, and love before the objectively worthy God of all.

Keep the faith teaching that ultimately evil will be punished and the world will be made right by the just Judge, and we who believe in Him will be made to stand by pure grace.

Keep *that* faith in the glorious God who alone is able to joyously keep us through the coming fire. As Jared Wilson writes of Jude's conclusion—and as we will explore further in the concluding reflections below—"We see in the end the radiance of glory that stands in stark contrast to the depths of wickedness."[22]

Concluding Reflections

Having studied the themes of lawlessness, irreverence, and licentiousness, along with mercy, peace, and love, complete the following sentences to personalize what has been learned.

Avoiding lawlessness multiplies mercy to me because:

Avoiding irreverence multiples peace to me because:

Avoiding licentiousness multiplies love to me because:

Read Jude 1 and 24–25. By Christ's power and for His sake, we transform into Christlikeness. As inspired by Jared Wilson noted above, consider the questions below concerning how His worth radiates by contrast with the wickedness of the world.

Not a hidden reef that slyly destructs without warning, who is the Lord according to Psalm 61:1–4 and Daniel 2:34–35, 44–45?

Not a shepherd who avoids feeding his sheep, who is the Lord according to Psalm 23:1 and John 10:11?

Not a waterless cloud with nothing to dispense, who is the Lord according to Hosea 6:3 and John 4:14?

Not a fruitless, uprooted tree, who is the Lord according to Isaiah 11:1 and 53:2 and John 15:5?

Not a wandering star that cannot be followed, who is Jesus according to Malachi 4:2, Revelation 22:16, and John 9:5?

As you reflect on these studies in Jude, how do you now think and believe differently about the following:

the connection between sound doctrine and your and others being kept?

the preciousness and urgency of truth and the importance of contending?

the worship you can offer to God for His grace in Christ?

the view you have of Christ's great authority, worth, and loveliness?

the joy and responsibility of your holy calling as a Christian?

the meaning of "keeping the faith"?

THE CHICAGO STATEMENT ON BIBLICAL INERRANCY[1]

A SHORT STATEMENT

1. God, who is Himself Truth and speaks truth only, has inspired Holy Scripture in order thereby to reveal Himself to lost mankind through Jesus Christ as Creator and Lord, Redeemer and Judge. Holy Scripture is God's witness to Himself.

2. Holy Scripture, being God's own Word, written by men prepared and superintended by His Spirit, is of infallible divine authority in all matters upon which it touches: it is to be believed, as God's instruction, in all that it affirms; obeyed, as God's command, in all that it requires; embraced, as God's pledge, in all that it promises.

3. The Holy Spirit, Scripture's divine Author, both authenticates it to us by His inward witness and opens our minds to understand its meaning.

4. Being wholly and verbally God-given, Scripture is without error or fault in all its teaching, no less in what it states about God's acts in creation, about the events of world history, and about its own literary origins under God, than in its witness to God's saving grace in individual lives.

5. The authority of Scripture is inescapably impaired if this total divine inerrancy is in any way limited or disregarded, or made relative to a view of truth contrary to the Bible's own; and such lapses bring serious loss to both the individual and the Church.

ARTICLES OF AFFIRMATION AND DENIAL

ARTICLE I

We affirm that the Holy Scriptures are to be received as the authoritative Word of God.

We deny that the Scriptures receive their authority from the Church, tradition, or any other human source.

ARTICLE II

We affirm that the Scriptures are the supreme written norm by which God binds the conscience, and that the authority of the Church is subordinate to that of Scripture.

We deny that Church creeds, councils, or declarations have authority greater than or equal to the authority of the Bible.

ARTICLE III

We affirm that the written Word in its entirety is revelation given by God.

We deny that the Bible is merely a witness to revelation, or only becomes revelation in encounter, or depends on the responses of men for its validity.

ARTICLE IV

We affirm that God who made mankind in His image has used language as a means of revelation.

We deny that human language is so limited by our creatureliness that it is rendered inadequate as a vehicle for divine revelation. We further deny that the corruption of human culture and language through sin has thwarted God's work of inspiration.

ARTICLE V

We affirm that God's revelation in the Holy Scriptures was progressive.

We deny that later revelation, which may fulfill earlier revelation, ever corrects or contradicts it. We further deny that any normative revelation has been given since the completion of the New Testament writings.

ARTICLE VI

We affirm that the whole of Scripture and all its parts, down to the very words of the original, were given by divine inspiration.

We deny that the inspiration of Scripture can rightly be affirmed of the whole without the parts, or of some parts but not the whole.

ARTICLE VII

We affirm that inspiration was the work in which God by His Spirit, through human writers, gave us His Word. The origin of Scripture is divine. The mode of divine inspiration remains largely a mystery to us.

We deny that inspiration can be reduced to human insight, or to heightened states of consciousness of any kind.

ARTICLE VIII

We affirm that God in His Work of inspiration utilized the distinctive personalities and literary styles of the writers whom He had chosen and prepared.

We deny that God, in causing these writers to use the very words that He chose, overrode their personalities.

ARTICLE IX

We affirm that inspiration, though not conferring omniscience, guaranteed true and trustworthy utterance on all matters of which the Biblical authors were moved to speak and write.

We deny that the finitude or fallenness of these writers, by necessity or otherwise, introduced distortion or falsehood into God's Word.

ARTICLE X

We affirm that inspiration, strictly speaking, applies only to the autographic text of Scripture, which in the providence of God can be ascertained from available manuscripts with great accuracy. We further affirm that copies and translations of Scripture are the Word of God to the extent that they faithfully represent the original.

We deny that any essential element of the Christian faith is affected by the absence of the autographs. We further deny that this absence renders the assertion of Biblical inerrancy invalid or irrelevant.

ARTICLE XI

We affirm that Scripture, having been given by divine inspiration, is infallible, so that, far from misleading us, it is true and reliable in all the matters it addresses.

We deny that it is possible for the Bible to be at the same time infallible and errant in its assertions. Infallibility and inerrancy may be distinguished, but not separated.

ARTICLE XII

We affirm that Scripture in its entirety is inerrant, being free from all falsehood, fraud, or deceit.

We deny that Biblical infallibility and inerrancy are limited to spiritual, religious, or redemptive themes, exclusive of assertions in the fields of history and science. We further deny that scientific hypotheses about earth history may properly be used to overturn the teaching of Scripture on creation and the flood.

ARTICLE XIII

We affirm the propriety of using inerrancy as a theological term with reference to the complete truthfulness of Scripture.

We deny that it is proper to evaluate Scripture according to standards of truth and error that are alien to its usage or purpose. We further deny that inerrancy is negated by Biblical phenomena such as a lack of modern technical precision, irregularities of grammar or spelling, observational descriptions of nature, the reporting of falsehoods, the use of hyperbole and round numbers, the topical arrangement of material, variant selections of material in parallel accounts, or the use of free citations.

ARTICLE XIV

We affirm the unity and internal consistency of Scripture.

We deny that alleged errors and discrepancies that have not yet been resolved vitiate the truth claims of the Bible.

ARTICLE XV

We affirm that the doctrine of inerrancy is grounded in the teaching of the Bible about inspiration.

We deny that Jesus' teaching about Scripture may be dismissed by appeals to accommodation or to any natural limitation of His humanity.

We affirm that the doctrine of inerrancy has been integral to the Church's faith throughout its history.

We deny that inerrancy is a doctrine invented by Scholastic Protestantism, or is a reactionary position postulated in response to negative higher criticism.

ARTICLE XVII

We affirm that the Holy Spirit bears witness to the Scriptures, assuring believers of the truthfulness of God's written Word.

We deny that this witness of the Holy Spirit operates in isolation from or against Scripture.

ARTICLE XVIII

We affirm that the text of Scripture is to be interpreted by grammatico-historical exegesis, taking account of its literary forms and devices, and that Scripture is to interpret Scripture.

We deny the legitimacy of any treatment of the text or quest for sources lying behind it that leads to relativizing, dehistoricizing, or discounting its teaching, or rejecting its claims to authorship.

ARTICLE XIX

We affirm that a confession of the full authority, infallibility, and inerrancy of Scripture is vital to a sound understanding of the whole of the Christian faith. We further affirm that such confession should lead to increasing conformity to the image of Christ.

We deny that such confession is necessary for salvation. However, we further deny that inerrancy can be rejected without grave consequences, both to the individual and to the Church.

ACKNOWLEDGMENTS

My heartfelt thanks to Gina Nunes, Pastor Brad Wetherell, and Beth Wetherell at The Orchard Evangelical Free Church in Itasca, Illinois: Gina Nunes for being a caring leader and inviting me to write the early version of this study for the women's ministry, Pastor Brad Wetherell for valuable thoughts on that first version, and Beth Wetherell who warmheartedly prompted me to seek the potential of publication for this study.

My heartfelt gratitude to Dr. Pam MacRae for her stimulating and wise mentorship, especially as a professor throughout my time studying at Moody Bible Institute, and for her ongoing relationship and encouragement of my writing.

I simply want to rave about the team at Moody Publishers in general and then, particularly those with whom I have had most direct contact, Judy Dunagan and Pam Pugh. In every communication with me, Scripture has driven the decisions in this publication process—what a joy as an author! Judy, my acquisitions editor, continually displays a commitment to writing and publishing being, first and foremost, a prayer-filled ministry for the glory of God and true blessing of others. For her sincere care for me and partnership, my deepest thanks. Pam's editorial expertise has carried this study into a brand-new dimension of usefulness for the reader, and I have learned much from her insights into this genre. The study has tremendously benefitted from her editorial feedback, corrections, and interaction. And when Judy said I would love working with her, she was right.

Abigail Priebe lent me her thoughtful editorial prowess on the proposal and first full draft of this manuscript. Meredith Hodge gave me redirecting and helpful reaction to the first week of the study. Thank you to these kind friends.

To my husband, Tyler, who consistently puts me ahead of himself and sees the aims on my heart as a family priority, my indebtedness. The first draft was bettered by his review and keen eye, and by the clarifying and Christ-exalting conversations on Jude's epistle we had together.

To my grandfather, Dr. David Hesselgrave, now with the Lord, belongs all my thanks for stirring in me a captivation for Jude's epistle and with "the faith," and for moving me to see their importance. Most of all, my gratitude belongs to him for earnestly and wholeheartedly living his firm biblical convictions until his final breath.

To my dear parents, whose love and wisdom were like a haven on earth during my growing up years, belong my immense gratitude for teaching me about truth, discernment, and love for Jesus Christ, and passing to me what was once passed to them—that which has already been delivered once-for-all to the saints.

NOTES

Introduction: What to Anticipate from Jude

1. According to Thomas Schreiner, Calvin held this view. Thomas R. Schreiner, *1, 2 Peter, Jude*, vol. 37, The New American Commentary (Nashville: Broadman & Holman, 2003), Logos ed., 404.

2. According to Hesselgrave and Hesselgrave, Jerome also held this view: David J. Hesselgrave and Ronald P. Hesselgrave, *What in the World Has Gotten into the Church?: Studies in the Book of Jude for Contemporary Christians* (Chicago: Moody, 1981), 20.

3. Louis Barbieri, "Jude," in *The Moody Bible Commentary,* Michael Rydelnik and Michael Vanlaningham, gen. eds. (Chicago: Moody, 2014), 1995.

Week One: Keeping in Truth

1. Ted Cabal, Chad Owen Brand, et al., *The Apologetics Study Bible: Real Questions, Straight Answers, Stronger Faith* (Nashville: Holman Bible Publishers, 2007), Logos ed., 1680.

2. R. Albert Mohler Jr., "Response," in *Beyond the Impasse?: Scripture, Interpretation, and Theology in Baptist Life*, Robinson B. James and David S. Dockery, eds. (Nashville: Broadman, 1992), 249, quoted in D. A. Carson, *The Gagging of God: Christianity Confronts Pluralism* (Grand Rapids: Zondervan, 2011), 353.

3. David S. Dockery and Timothy George, *The Great Tradition of Christian Thinking: A Student's Guide* (Wheaton, IL: Crossway, 2012), Kindle ed., location nos. 976–79.

4. David J. Hesselgrave and Ronald P. Hesselgrave, *What in the World Has Gotten into the Church?: Studies in the Book of Jude for Contemporary Christians* (Chicago: Moody, 1981), 17.

5. Some of the founding members were evangelical leaders such as Francis Schaeffer, R. C. Sproul, J. I. Packer, John MacArthur, James Montgomery Boice, Carl F. H. Henry, and D. A. Carson. You can read about this council at "Records of the International Council on Biblical Inerrancy," https://library.dts.edu/Pages/TL/Special/ICBI.shtml.

6. These articles are available at http://theapologeticsgroup.com/wp-content/uploads/2012/06/42_Articles_Christian_Worldview.pdf and also are in Jay Grimstead and Eugene Calvin Clingman, *Rebuilding Civilization on the Bible: Proclaiming the Truth on 24 Controversial Issues* (Ventura, CA: Nordskog, 2014), 36–42.

7. Johannes P. Louw and Eugene Albert Nida, *Greek-English Lexicon of the New Testament: Based on Semantic Domains* (New York: United Bible Societies, 1996), 475.

8. J. N. D. Kelly, *A Commentary on the Epistles of Peter and of Jude* (Grand Rapids: Baker Book House, 1969), Logos ed., 242.

9. Ibid., 242.

10. Hesselgrave and Hesselgrave, *What in the World Has Gotten into the Church?*, 18.

11. Charles Wesley, "And Can It Be, That I Should Gain?," Hymnary.org, 2019, https://hymnary .org/text/and_can_it_be_that_i_should_gain.

Week Two: Keeping in Grace

1. D. A. Carson, *Exegetical Fallacies*, 2nd ed., (Grand Rapids: Baker Academic, 1996), 89.

2. Thomas R. Schreiner, *1, 2 Peter, Jude*, vol. 37, The New American Commentary (Nashville: Broadman & Holman, 2003), Logos ed., 436.

3. Michael W. Holmes, *The Apostolic Fathers: Greek Texts and English Translations*, updated ed. (Grand Rapids: Baker Books, 1999), 142.

4. J. C. Connell, "Gentleness" in *New Bible Dictionary*, D. R. W. Wood, I. H. Marshall, A. R. Millard, J. I. Packer, and D. J. Wiseman, eds. (Leicester, England; Downers Grove, IL: InterVarsity, 1996), 405.

5. John Calvin, *Commentary on Psalms—Volume 1* (Grand Rapids: Christian Classics Ethereal Library, n.d.), 34, https://www.ccel.org/ccel/calvin/calcom08.pdf.

6. *Ante-Nicene Fathers: Volume 1 The Apostolic Fathers, Justin Martyr, Irenaeus*, Philip Schaff, ed. (Grand Rapids: Christian Classics Ethereal Library, n.d.), 842, http://www.ccel.org/ccel/schaff/ anf01.pdf.

7. John MacArthur, *2 Peter and Jude*, MacArthur New Testament Commentary (Chicago: Moody, 2005), Logos ed., 159. Emphasis in original.

8. Matthew Henry, *Matthew Henry's Commentary on the Whole Bible: Complete and Unabridged in One Volume* (Peabody, MA: Hendrickson, 1994), Logos ed., 990.

9. Schreiner, *1, 2 Peter, Jude*, 438.

10. Ibid., 437.

11. Charles Hodge, *Systematic Theology* (Oak Harbor, WA: Logos Research Systems, 1997), Logos ed., 3:122.

12. If you would like to examine this point further, see: Richard J. Bauckham, *Jude–2 Peter*, vol. 50 (Word Biblical Commentary), eds. David A. Hubbard and Glenn W. Barker (Dallas: Word, 1998), 40; Schreiner, *1, 2 Peter, Jude*, 413; Douglas J. Moo, *The NIV Application Commentary: 2 Peter and Jude* (Grand Rapids: Zondervan, 1996), 245; and Peter H. Davids, *The Letters of 2 Peter and Jude,* The Pillar New Testament Commentary (Grand Rapids: Eerdmans, 2006), Logos ed., 58.

13. David J. Hesselgrave and Ronald P. Hesselgrave, *What in the World Has Gotten into the Church?: Studies in the Book of Jude for Contemporary Christians* (Chicago: Moody, 1981), 72.

14. Ibid.

15. Ibid., 19.

16. H. A. Ironside, *An Exposition of the Epistle of Jude* (Neptune, NJ: Loizeaux Brothers, 1931), Logos ed., 14.

17. Douglas J. Moo, *The NIV Application Commentary: 2 Peter and Jude* (Grand Rapids: Zondervan, 1996), Logos ed., 237.

18. Martin Luther, "Lord, Keep Us Steadfast in Thy Word," trans. Catherine Winkworth, Hymnary .org, https://hymnary.org/text/lord_keep_us_steadfast_in_your_word.

19. Gene L. Green, *Jude and 2 Peter:* Baker Exegetical Commentary on the New Testament (Grand Rapids: Baker Academic, 2008), 49.

20. J. N. D. Kelly, *A Commentary on the Epistles of Peter and Jude* (Grand Rapids: Baker Book House, 1969), Logos ed., 244.

21. Green, *Jude and 2 Peter,* 49.

22. Hesselgrave and Hesselgrave, *What in the World Has Gotten into the Church?*, 25.

Week Three: Keeping the Soul

1. Quote and chart adapted from Hesselgrave and Hesselgrave, *What in the World Has Gotten into the Church?: Studies in the Book of Jude for Contemporary Christians* (Chicago: Moody, 1981), 64–65.

2. David J. Hesselgrave, "Challenging the Church to World Mission," *International Journal of Frontier Missions* 13, no. 2 (1996): 30.

3. Sinclair B. Ferguson, *The Whole Christ: Legalism, Antinomianism, and Gospel Assurance—Why the Marrow Controversy Still Matters* (Wheaton, IL: Crossway, 2016), 169.

4. Hesselgrave and Hesselgrave, *What in the World Has Gotten into the Church?*, 64.

5. Some commentators note that "Jesus" is most prevalent in the manuscripts; while "Lord" is seen less frequently in the manuscripts, others believe "Lord" was in the original. Commentator Davids's analysis is that Jude seems to have Jesus in mind, intending to communicate that Jesus Himself will bring unbelievers to destruction. Peter H. Davids, *The Letters of 2 Peter and Jude,* The Pillar New Testament Commentary (Grand Rapids: Eerdmans, 2006), Logos ed., 48.

6. Martin Luther, *The Epistles of St. Peter and St. Jude: Preached and Explained,* ed. and trans. by John Nicholas Lenker in *The Precious and Sacred Writings of Martin Luther* (Minneapolis, MN: Lutherans in All Lands Co., 1904), Logos ed., 372.

7. Charles Haddon Spurgeon, *Spurgeon's Sermons Volume 41: 1895* (Grand Rapids: Christian Classics Ethereal Library, n.d.), 234, https://www.ccel.org/ccel/spurgeon/sermons41.pdf.

8. According to D. A. Carson and G. K. Beale, *Commentary on the New Testament Use of the Old Testament* (Grand Rapids: Baker Academic, 2007), 1072.

9. For a more in-depth discussion on this, see ibid., 1070–72.

10. Thomas R. Schreiner, *1, 2 Peter, Jude*, vol. 37, The New American Commentary (Nashville: Broadman & Holman, 2003), Logos ed., 448.

11. Peter H. Davids, *The Letters of 2 Peter and Jude,* The Pillar New Testament Commentary (Grand Rapids: Eerdmans, 2006), Logos ed., 50.

12. *The Holman Illustrated Bible,* Chad Brand et al., eds. (Nashville: Holman Bible, 2003), 397.

13. Gene L. Green, *Jude and 2 Peter:* Baker Exegetical Commentary on the New Testament (Grand Rapids: Baker Academic, 2008), 92.

14. Charles Haddon Spurgeon, *Spurgeon's Sermons Volume 08: 1862* (Grand Rapids: Christian Classics Ethereal Library, n.d.), 411, http://www.ccel.org/ccel/spurgeon/sermons08.pdf.

15. Josephus writes: "Now Corah, when he said this, had a mind to appear to take care of the public welfare; but in reality he was endeavoring to procure to have that dignity transferred by the multitude to himself. Thus did he, out of a malignant design, but with plausible words, discourse to those of his own tribe" (Josephus Flavius, *The Works of Josephus: Complete and Unabridged*, trans. William Whiston [Peabody: Hendrickson, 1987], 103).

16. Charles Wesley, "Depth of Mercy! can there be," Hymnary.org, https://hymnary.org/text/depth_of_mercy_can_there_be.

Week Four: Keeping the Spirit

1. David Wells, *God in the Whirlwind: How the Holy-love of God Reorients Our World* (Wheaton, IL: Crossway, 2014), Kindle ed., location no. 630.

2. Martin H. Manser, *Dictionary of Bible Themes: The Accessible and Comprehensive Tool for Topical Studies* (London: Martin Manser, 2009), Logos ed., entry no. 5896.

3. David J. Hesselgrave and Ronald P. Hesselgrave, *What in the World Has Gotten into the Church?: Studies in the Book of Jude for Contemporary Christians* (Chicago: Moody, 1981), 64–65.

4. Irenaeus, "The Demonstration of the Apostolic Preaching," ccel.org, para. 71, http://www.ccel.org/ccel/irenaeus/demonstr.iv.html#iv-p64.8.

5. Wells, *God in the Whirlwind*, location no. 517.

6. Ibid., location no. 274.

7. Ibid., location no. 3131.

8. Ibid., location no. 514.

9. Hesselgrave and Hesselgrave, *What in the World Has Gotten into the Church?*, 64. The prophecy of Enoch is not included in this chart since the authors treat that topic separately.

10. John MacArthur, *2 Peter and Jude*, MacArthur New Testament Commentary (Chicago: Moody, 2005), Logos ed., 179.

11. Thomas R. Schreiner, *1, 2 Peter, Jude*, vol. 37, The New American Commentary (Nashville: Broadman & Holman, 2003), Logos ed., 465.

12. Hesselgrave and Hesselgrave, *What in the World Has Gotten into the Church?*, 34.

13. Peter H. Davids, *The Letters of 2 Peter and Jude,* The Pillar New Testament Commentary (Grand Rapids: Eerdmans, 2006), Logos ed., 60.

14. MacArthur, *2 Peter and Jude*, 176.

15. Crossway Bibles, *The ESV Study Bible* (Wheaton, IL: Crossway Bibles, 2008), 1755.

16. Hesselgrave and Hesselgrave, *What in the World Has Gotten into the Church?*, 35.

17. See, for examples, H. A. Ironside, *An Exposition of the Epistle of Jude* (Neptune, NJ: Loizeaux Brothers, 1931), 31–32; and MacArthur, *2 Peter and Jude*, 177.

18. Davids, *The Letters of 2 Peter and Jude*, 65.

19. D. A. Carson and G. K. Beale, eds., *Commentary on the New Testament Use of the Old Testament* (Grand Rapids: Baker Academic, 2007), 1076.

20. Douglas J. Moo, *The NIV Application Commentary: 2 Peter and Jude* (Grand Rapids: Zondervan, 1996), Logos ed., 256.

21. C. F. Keil and F. Delitzsch, *Biblical Commentary on the Old Testament*, trans. James Martin (Edinburgh: T. & T. Clark, 1885), 110, https://archive.org/details/BiblicalCommentaryOld Testament.KeilAndDelitzsch.6/page/n113.

22. David J. Hesselgrave, "Challenging the Church to World Mission," *International Journal of Frontier Missions* 13, no. 2 (1996): 35.

23. Robert Harvey and Philip H. Towner, *2 Peter & Jude* in The IVP New Testament Commentary Series, ed. Grant R. Osborne, vol. 18 (Downers Grove, IL; Nottingham, England: InterVarsity, 2009), Logos ed., 204.

24. T. Desmond Alexander, *From Eden to the New Jerusalem: An Introduction to Biblical Theology* (Grand Rapids: Kregel Academic, 2008), 107.

25. Ibid.

26. This quote is not in the Bible, but it is similar to what is written in a book called *1 Enoch,* or the *Book of Enoch.* Concerning the source of the quotation in Jude, commentator R. C. H. Lenski writes: "Jude quotes Enoch and not some book. How well or ill or in what manner the *Book of Enoch* reproduces Enoch's prophecy is a minor matter and does not affect Jude. Jude quotes directly; whether the *Book of Enoch* quotes directly or indirectly—what difference does it make? Jude and the *Book of Enoch* say about the same thing; but that lends nothing to Jude, nor does it detract from him" (R. C. H. Lenski, *The Interpretation of the Epistles of St. Peter, St. John and St. Jude* [Minneapolis: Augsburg Publishing House, 1966], Logos ed., 641–42).

27. Anonymous, "Come to the Ark," Hymnary.org, https://hymnary.org/text/come_to_the_ark_ come_to_the_ark.

28. Mark Dever, *The Message of the Old Testament: Promises Made* (Wheaton, IL: Crossway Books, 2006), 71.

29. Jared C. Wilson, "Jude," in *The ESV Gospel Transformation Bible*, Bryan Chapell, gen. ed. (Wheaton, IL: Crossway, 2013), 1723.

30. Anonymous, "Come to the Ark."

Week Five: Keeping the Body

1. Robert Duncan Culver, *Systematic Theology: Biblical and Historical* (Ross-shire, UK: Mentor, 2005), 1075.

2. Ibid.

3. S. Lewis Johnson, *Discovering Romans: Spiritual Revival for the Soul* (Grand Rapids: Zondervan, 2014), Kindle ed., 31.

4. Chart adopted from David J. Hesselgrave and Ronald P. Hesselgrave, *What in the World Has Gotten into the Church?: Studies in the Book of Jude for Contemporary Christians* (Chicago: Moody, 1981).

5. Culver, *Systematic Theology*, 1075.

6. Hesselgrave and Hesselgrave, *What in the World Has Gotten into the Church?*, 45. Emphasis in original.

7. Ibid., 64.

8. C. S. Lewis, *The Great Divorce* (1946; repr., New York: HarperOne, 2001), 72. Citations refer to the 2001 ed.

9. Peter H. Davids, *The Letters of 2 Peter and Jude,* The Pillar New Testament Commentary (Grand Rapids: Eerdmans, 2006), Logos ed., 55.

10. Carl F. H. Henry, *Toward a Recovery of Christian Belief: The Rutherford Lectures* (Wheaton, IL: Crossway Books, 1990), 40.

11. Ibid.

12. Ibid.*,* 28.

13. John MacArthur, *2 Peter and Jude*, MacArthur New Testament Commentary (Chicago: Moody, 2005), Logos ed., 180.

14. Ibid., 181. Emphasis in original.

15. Charles Haddon Spurgeon, *Spurgeon's Sermons Volume 11: 1865* (Grand Rapids: Christian Classics Ethereal Library, n.d.), 321, http://www.ccel.org/ccel/spurgeon/sermons11.pdf.

16. The most natural reading of Genesis 19:4–7 is that beyond hospitality, homosexual relations are being sought. Using "know" to refer to sexual relations not only has this immediate contextual support, but also support from elsewhere in Genesis. Michel G. Wechsler explains that "The word 'know' is frequently used in Genesis for sexual behavior (4:1, 17, 25; 24:16; 38:26)" (Michael G. Wechsler, "Genesis," in *The Moody Bible Commentary*, Michael Rydelnik and Michael Vanlaningham, gen. eds. [Chicago: Moody, 2014], 76). Given that usage, one interpretation of the sins of Sodom referenced in Jude 7 is that the men desired "other flesh" (*sarkos heteras* in the Greek) in a sense that meant the flesh of the angels. However, "the men in Sodom who had a sexual desire for the angels *did not know they were angels*" (Thomas R. Schreiner, *1, 2 Peter, Jude*, vol. 37, The New American Commentary [Nashville: Broadman & Holman, 2003], Logos ed., 453; emphasis in original. For a more in-depth, historical discussion, view Schreiner, *1, 2 Peter, Jude*, 452–53).

17. According to Moo, Jude's writing pattern demonstrates this to be a peak point in his letter:

"Jude does not follow the canonical order in the three examples he lists [in Jude 5–7]. Had he done so, we would have expected the angels' sin to come first (Gen. 6), Sodom and Gomorrah second (Gen. 19), and the desert generation third (Num. 14). But by following the order he does, Jude achieves a crescendo in punishment—from physical death (v. 5) to binding in darkness (v. 6) to the 'punishment of eternal fire'" (The *NIV Application Commentary: 2 Peter and Jude*, 243).

18. More Amorite kings were defeated under Joshua's leadership; see Joshua 10:6–10.

19. Sherri Youngward, "She Looks to the Sky," sherriyoungward.com, http://www.sherriyoungward .com/journal/she-looks-to-the-sky-journal. Used with permission.

20. Jonathan Edwards, *The Works of Jonathan Edwards, Volume One* (Grand Rapids: Christian Classics Ethereal Library, n.d.), 68, http://www.ccel.org/ccel/edwards/works1.pdf.

21. Ibid., 25.

22. Ibid., 67.

23. Sherri Youngward, "She Looks to the Sky."

24. Murray J. Harris, *The Second Epistle to the Corinthians: A Commentary on the Greek Text*, New International Greek Testament Commentary (Grand Rapids: Eerdmans; Paternoster Press, 2005), 419.

25. Edwards, *The Works of Jonathan Edwards*, 67.

26. Ibid., 25.

Week Six: He Is Able to Keep Us

1. Thomas C. Oden, *Agenda for Theology* (San Francisco: Harper and Row, 1979), 11.

2. See Douglas Moo, *The NIV Application Commentary: 2 Peter and Jude*, 233. Thomas Schreiner is unconvinced that Jude wrote intentionally conforming to this Greek pattern of writing but finds Watson's case helpful for analyzing Jude's structure. Thomas R. Schreiner, *1, 2 Peter, Jude*, vol. 37, The New American Commentary (Nashville: Broadman & Holman, 2003), Logos ed., 420. Commentators Moo (*The NIV Application Commentary: 2 Peter and Jude*, 232) and Davids (*The Letters of 2 Peter and Jude*, 24) are more convinced.

3. Douglas J. Moo, *The NIV Application Commentary: 2 Peter and Jude* (Grand Rapids: Zondervan, 1996), Logos ed., 233.

4. Peter H. Davids, *The Letters of 2 Peter and Jude*, The Pillar New Testament Commentary (Grand Rapids: Eerdmans, 2006), Logos ed., 24.

5. Moo, *The NIV Application Commentary: 2 Peter and Jude*, 232.

6. Gene L. Green, *Jude and 2 Peter:* Baker Exegetical Commentary on the New Testament (Grand Rapids: Baker Academic, 2008), 117.

7. Davids, *The Letters of 2 Peter and Jude*, 24.

8. Moo, *The NIV Application Commentary: 2 Peter and Jude*, 280.

9. "Doxology," in *Holman Illustrated Bible Dictionary*, Chad Brand, Charles Draper, Archie England, Steve Bond, E. Ray Clendenen, and Trent C. Butler, eds. (Nashville: Holman Bible, 2003), 441.

10. Schreiner understands "stumbling" (*aptaistous*) to refer to a final fall: "In Rom 11:11, however, the verb 'stumble' refers to whether the Jews have stumbled irrevocably, so that they will be lost forever. Paul answered that question with an emphatic no! Peter used the verbal form of this word in reference to apostasy in 2 Pet 1:10. And that is how Jude used the adjective here" (*1, 2 Peter, Jude*, 491).

11. Charles Haddon Spurgeon, *Spurgeon's Sermons Volume 59: 1913* (Grand Rapids: Christian Classics Ethereal Library, n.d.), 327–28, http://www.ccel.org/ccel/spurgeon/sermons59.pdf.

12. Davids, *The Letters of 2 Peter and Jude*, 110.

13. Ibid., 110.

14. Charles Haddon Spurgeon, *Spurgeon's Sermons Volume 11: 1865* (Grand Rapids: Christian Classics Ethereal Library, n.d.), 321, http://www.ccel.org/ccel/spurgeon/sermons11.pdf., emphasis added.

15. Ibid., emphasis added.

16. Ibid., 326, emphasis added.

17. According to Robert Culver, "Yet there will be loss of rewards which can only be gained in the present life by proper stewardship of God's gifts of abilities, of time and of strength through the Spirit (1 Cor. 3:12–15). I have already tried to show that we should not think of this scene as taking place at the Last Judgment, described as before 'a great white throne' (Rev. 20:11–15) following the millennium. Believers will not stand before God to be judged by Him in that grand assize, because they are to be associated with God in Christ at that judgment in some unspecified way. Paul says, 'the world is to be judged by you' (1 Cor. 6:2), including angels (1 Cor. 6:3)" (Robert Duncan Culver, *Systematic Theology: Biblical and Historical* [Ross-shire, UK: Mentor, 2005], 1070).

18. Culver, *Systematic Theology*, 1070.

19. Ibid.

20. Jonathan Edwards, *Charity and Its Fruits* (Edinburgh: Banner of Truth Trust, 1969), 164.

21. David J. Hesselgrave and Ronald P. Hesselgrave, *What in the World Has Gotten into the Church?: Studies in the Book of Jude for Contemporary Christians* (Chicago: Moody, 1981), 140. Emphasis in original.

22. Jared C. Wilson, "Jude," in *The ESV Gospel Transformation Bible*, Bryan Chapell, gen. ed. (Wheaton, IL: Crossway, 2013), 1723.

Appendix

1. International Council on Biblical Inerrancy, "The Chicago Statement on Biblical Inerrancy," https://library.dts.edu/Pages/TL/Special/ICBI_1.pdf. Used with the permission of the Alliance for Confessing Evangelicals.

Bible Studies for Women

IN-DEPTH. CHRIST-CENTERED. REAL IMPACT.

**AN UNEXPLAINABLE
LIFE**
978-0-8024-1473-1

**THE UNEXPLAINABLE
CHURCH**
978-0-8024-1742-8

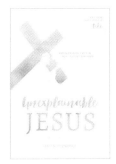

**UNEXPLAINABLE
JESUS**
978-0-8024-1909-5

HIS LAST WORDS
978-0-8024-1467-0

I AM FOUND
978-0-8024-1468-7

INCLUDED IN CHRIST
978-0-8024-1591-2

THIS I KNOW
978-0-8024-1596-7

**WHO DO YOU SAY
THAT I AM?**
978-0-8024-1550-9

HE IS ENOUGH
978-0-8024-1686-5

IF GOD IS FOR US
978-0-8024-1713-8

ON BENDED KNEE
978-0-8024-1919-4

Moody Publishers®

From the Word to Life

Explore our Bible studies at
moodypublisherswomen.com

Also available as eBooks

Experiencing the Joy of Personal Revival

Seeking Him is a 12-week interactive study on personal revival, for both groups and individuals. Get ready to experience the freedom and joy of an honest and humble heart, true repentance, God's amazing grace, genuine holiness, a clear conscience, radical forgiveness, sexual purity, and walking in the Spirit.

978-0-8024-1456-4 | also available as an eBook

MOODY
Publishers

From the Word to Life